GIRLFRIENDS'
GeTawaY

A COMPLETE GUIDE

to the Weekend Adventure That Turns Friends

into Sisters and Sisters into Friends

GIRLFRIENDS' Getaway

KATHLEEN LAING & ELIZABETH BUTTERFIELD

WATERBROOK
PRESS

GIRLFRIENDS' GETAWAY

PUBLISHED BY WATERBROOK PRESS

2375 Telstar Drive, Suite 160

Colorado Springs, Colorado 80920

A division of Random House, Inc.

All Scripture quotations, unless otherwise indicated, are taken from the *Holy Bible, New International Version*®. NIV®. Copyright © 1973, 1978, 1984 by International Bible Society. Used by permission of Zondervan Publishing House. All rights reserved. Scripture quotations marked (TLB) are taken from *The Living Bible* copyright ©1971. Used by permission of Tyndale House Publishers, Inc., Wheaton, Illinois 60189. All rights reserved.

ISBN 1-57856-516-2

Printed in the United States of America

2002—First Edition

10 9 8 7 6 5 4 3 2 1

To all Girlfriends, past, present, and future:
May your pursuit of sistering be a true adventure.

Contents

Acknowledgments ix

Introduction: *An Invitation with Your Name on It* 1

PART I: GET INSPIRED

One: The Adventure Begins 11

Two: Discover Your Girlfriends 25

Three: Set Up Camp 43

PART II: GET PACKING

Four: Follow the Map 61

Five: Stop for Lemonade 79

Six: Dig for Treasure 89

Seven: Diamond or Lump of Coal? 105

PART III: GET GOING

Eight: Enjoy the Riches 121

Nine: Share the Wealth 131

Epilogue: *The Adventure Continues* 147

Appendixes: *Girlfriends' Getaway Resources* 151

Notes 177

Acknowledgments

It's difficult to begin an acknowledgment of a work that involved so many people coming in at the right time to help make this book possible. Whom should we name first? If we really want to go to the source, we must first thank the woman who started our own Getaway tradition.

To Del: You had the vision and the desire to spend time with your daughters and granddaughters but probably never imagined just how large your vision would become. Thank you for your courage in beginning it all. We love you.

What would a Sisters Weekend be without the sisters? To Penny, Melodee, Terri, Peggy, Jessica, Jennie, Kate, Ann, Stephanie, and Caitlin: Thank you for sistering us throughout this process and for your continued support, ideas, insights, love, and prayers.

A special thank-you to our Jennie. Your passionate spirit and wisdom have brought a new dimension to all our lives. We look forward to your next adventure!

To our friend Jane Struck: Thank you for being a cheerleader when we needed it and for helping this book get into the right hands.

Thanks to our editor, Ron Lee, for your tireless enthusiasm and expertise. Despite the fact that you're not a Girlfriend, you caught the vision and understood the value of this concept. We were "tracking" right from the beginning!

Thank you to all our wonderful Girlfriends—you know who you are. We felt your love and encouragement from day one.

To all the women who generously shared your stories: Thank you for helping us show that a Girlfriends' Getaway is an adventure for *all* women.

And finally, to our husbands, Craig and Kirk: Thank you for not laughing at us when we said we were going to write a book and for being our biggest fans ever since. We knew there was a reason we married you guys!

an invitation
WITH YOUR name on IT

This invitation is just for you. Well, for you and your closest girl-friends, of course. If you accept, you'll be in for an adventure of fun, support, and enrichment. It's yours for the taking right here in this little book. The concept of a Girlfriends' Getaway, a break from your normal routines so you can spend time with special women in your life, is ours to offer and yours to create. Although the idea of setting your schedule aside to enjoy a getaway with your friends or sisters may be new to you, we've got a feeling that it's something you've been wanting and needing for a long, long time.

No one, other than God, understands women like other women. Who else, if not our girlfriends, really gets it? In our daily lives, it seems that everyone wants something from us. We keep our families organized and our homes running smoothly. We keep our offices professional and our cell phones on. We work long hours, both in the home and outside it. But not only do we take care of the details of daily life, we often carry the emotional load in our families as well, trying to keep everyone strong and positive in a sometimes scary world. We wear so many hats that we sometimes feel we lost track of the details a long time ago.

If anyone needs a weekend just for you, it's, well, you.

That's why we wrote this book. It's a practical guide that will give you everything you need to pull off your own Girlfriends' Getaway. Don't hyperventilate; it's really not that big of a deal. You don't have to set aside an entire weekend, and even though we call it an adventure, you don't need to travel to an exotic location. You can start with something as small as a coffee break and eventually work up to a more elaborate experience. While the details vary with every group, one element is nonnegotiable: spending meaningful time with the women you love the most, or even the women you'll *grow* to love the most. They are the "Girlfriends" referred to in *Girlfriends' Getaway*.

Your chosen girlfriends can be the women you've known since birth, your actual sisters. They can be the friends you've grown closest to over the years, or even friends with whom you'd like to develop a closer bond. A girlfriend is who *you* say she is.

Take us, for example. We started our connection in the closest way imaginable—we are mother (Kathleen) and daughter (Elizabeth). But we also enjoy a woman-to-woman relationship that has developed into a deep friendship. At this point in our lives, we are blessed to be girlfriends in the best and most complete sense of the word.

THE GLORY OF GIRLFRIENDS

You may be wondering, *But what if I don't have a sister or any really close friends?* Trust us. Even if you're an only child, we bet you have at least one friend. And probably many more. If you still can't think of any, we've got some tips for finding girlfriends in the most unexpected places. Don't worry—they're there, either inside your family or somewhere very near.

Perhaps you have sisters, or even plenty of girlfriends, but no time. Who does? You'll *find* the time once you realize how much you need the rewards of this special getaway. Before we dive into the details, let's consider the power we possess. Women joining together—whether in a family, a church, or a community—create a human bond like few others. It's no accident that those in the building trades use the word *sistering* to describe the process of nailing one board to another in order to strengthen the first where it is weak. In joining two boards side-by-side, both pieces are made stronger. The new "sistered" boards can now bear a much heavier load because they each benefit from the other's strength.

We couldn't have invented a better image. Are you carrying a load you feel you simply can't handle any longer? You need to be sistered. Are the needs and demands of those closest to you draining your last ounce of energy? You need the strength that comes through the circle of sisterhood. Are the concerns of family, work, and life in general keeping you from enjoying peace of mind? In that case, you need the sanity of sisters. Has it been way too long since you've done something just for the fun of doing it? We hear you, and so do your closest friends. Your girlfriends are carrying the same load, and they need a break just as much as you do. So why not bring them together and go for it?

The Doable Adventure

We'll show you how easy it is to pull off a Girlfriends' Getaway adventure. Whether it's a weekend, a Saturday morning, or a weekday evening, this is a special time just for you and your friends. It's a chance for women to come alongside one another to share their lives, to lift one another up, and to strengthen one another. It's also a chance to let your hair down and enjoy a lot of fun. There are no cell phones chirping, no pagers vibrating, no bosses demanding a report by tomorrow morning. Gone for the moment are kids with a science project they forgot to tell you about, sick pets making a mess on the carpet, and golf-obsessed husbands, and overheated boyfriends, and to-do lists, and piles of laundry, and… Excuse us while we step outside and scream.

Okay, we're back. Sorry if we got carried away.

A Girlfriends' Getaway isn't about rushing around to meet the needs of all the people who depend on you. It's about your need to bond with other women and their need to bond with you. You can relax around one another, be yourself, and touch one another's lives. While it won't solve *all* your problems, you'll be amazed at how far a little love, laughter, and support can take you. It's the strength that comes through sistering.

Let us tell you a bit about our own journey. In 1990 my mother, my sisters, and I (Kathleen) launched an annual adventure we call Sisters Weekend. Different name, same concept. Actually, the name came easily, since we spent a weekend together, and the first few getaways involved only five sisters and our mother. That first year we crowded into a single hotel room, all six of us. The space was tight, and sometimes we tripped over one another. But we left for home at the end of our first adventure already making plans for the following year. We haven't missed a getaway since.

In recent years our circle has grown to include three generations: a mother, her daughters, and now *their* young-adult daughters, Elizabeth among them. We've supported one another through times of crisis, loss, and heartache. We've hugged and prayed and cried together. We've learned things from and about one another. We've also cooked up some of the craziest "girls having fun" adventures known to humankind. And we've laughed together until tears streamed down our faces.

After benefiting from the richness of these shared weekends, we decided that we can't keep it to ourselves any longer. We want you to experience this adventure for yourself.

Already, women across the country are developing their own expressions of the Girlfriends' Getaway adventure. There are as many names for it as there are women who love it. There's Estrofest, for example, an annual weekend that brings sisters, daughters, and cousins together from Virginia to San Francisco. These women celebrate their shared heritage as only a family of women could. Then there is the Wrestling Team of suburban Chicago, a group of women who spend time together sorting out the various life struggles they're facing. And we don't want to overlook the Shady Ladies, a group of friends from California who have spent blissful weekends together sharing their love of quilting while relaxing at their favorite lake. The stories of these and other groups will appear throughout this book to show how women are reaching out to their girlfriends—sisters, cousins, daughters, longtime friends, newfound friends—and to show that pulling it off isn't as difficult as it might seem.

EXTENDING THE BLESSINGS

Spending time with our girlfriends does more than just strengthen the women in the group. It also radiates out to affect everyone whose lives we touch. Our husbands, children, coworkers, and neighbors all benefit from the improved version of *us* that results from spending meaningful time with our girlfriends. The Girlfriends' Getaway experience leaves us feeling good about who we are as women. The result is confidence and energy to invest ourselves more fully in the lives of others.

As you can see, we're sold on the idea. But let's say you've already tried to get some close friends, or your actual sisters, together, and somehow things just didn't gel. Maybe you're reluctant to give it another try, fearing that you'll just invite further misunderstanding or frustration. The last thing you want is to endure a weekend of women grumbling about the food, the activities, or the lodging. Well, we don't have a foolproof formula. But with a little advance planning and the right expectations, you can launch into this adventure with confidence that the rewards will far outweigh the risks involved. That's *almost* a money-back guarantee.

A Girlfriends' Getaway is a time for authenticity. We drop our labels the moment we get together. There are no moms, firstborns, best friends, mere acquaintances, aunts, or daughters. As women banding together for mutual support and outlandish fun, we are equals. We are free to be silly if we want, and we're free to honestly share our hearts. We are free to be vulnerable, to open up, to help, and to be helped. It's a time for slowing down, pushing away the stresses of the world, and regrouping so that we're stronger when we reenter the fray of daily life. We come away refreshed and renewed, ready to slip back into our roles with a fresh perspective. After a Girlfriends' Getaway adventure, we are better able to look at our lives with gratitude.

Time to Get Started

To make this book as easy to use as possible, we've broken it into three parts. Part 1, "Get Inspired," begins with you. It's designed to help you catch a vision for creating your own getaway adventure. We'll help you identify the areas of your life, including your interior life, that will be nurtured by the Girlfriends' Getaway experience. We hope the stories you read will get you excited about planning your first adventure, and soon!

Part 2, "Get Packing," shows you how to start pulling it all together. We wouldn't blame you for feeling overwhelmed at the thought of cramming yet another activity into your bursting schedule. And even if you had the time, how in the world could you get a group of women to agree on a date, a location, and things to do together? Excellent questions, by the way. Continue reading and we'll give you the answers. We'll show you how to identify your "Girlfriends." We'll explain how to handle the planning and how to cover all the logistics of schedules, lodging, finances, child care, time off from work, and much more.

Finally, part 3, "Get Going," sends you off on your first Girlfriends' Getaway and provides ideas for activities you might want to try once you get there. Your adventure can be as impulsive or as structured as you want. We've done everything from skits, song-and-dance routines, games, and outings to do-it-yourself day spas and inventive dining experiences. They have all created lasting memories. We've also dropped all our plans and simply headed off to do whatever occurred to us at the moment. It all works when you approach it with the right attitude and with realistic expectations. So to gain exposure to a wide array of great things you can do with your girlfriends, turn to part 3.

If you're already sold on the idea and want to hurry and get started (in which case you're probably not reading this introduction anyway), just skim the sidebars in part 1 and then dig into part 2. The sidebars throughout the book are labeled according to the help they offer. The K.I.S.S. sidebars show you how to "keep it simple, sister." The Bumps and Bruises sidebars explain problems you'll want to avoid. (We've already made the mistakes so you don't have to!) The sidebars labeled A Closer Look suggest interesting moments you could create during the Girlfriends' Getaway adventure. The Getaway Gear sidebars suggest creative, useful, and sometimes outlandish accessories that will enhance your getaway experience. And the Remedies sidebars provide a dose of lively fun to cure the lackluster getaway. These sidebars provide ideas that add spark, life, and sometimes a laugh or two—just what you need to keep your getaway running at full strength.

The space provided in the Field Notes section is a place where you can write down your questions and great ideas as they occur to you. You won't want to lose any of the possibilities as you prepare for your own special adventure.

We hope you're ready, because it's time to begin the adventure.

PART I | GET INSPIRED

Chapter 1

THE ADVENTURE BEGINS

Whatever you can dream you can do—begin it.
Boldness has genius, power, and magic. Begin it now!
—JOHANN WOLFGANG VON GOETHE

Welcome, girlfriend! We're thrilled to have you join us in the adventure that has enriched the lives of women from every walk of life, from every region of the country, of all ages, and from all backgrounds. These women have young children, grown children, and no children. They're single, married, or somewhere in between. They go to an office every day, they're in school, they work full-time at home. They represent women in all of our rich diversity, but they have one crucial thing in common: They gain incredible strength, wisdom, and encouragement from one another.

The women who gather for these special getaways do bold, adventurous things together. They open their lives to one another, they care for one another, and they forge bonds that all women want, but too few ever know. We're glad you're here, because we know you're this type of woman.

But before we plunge in, we want you to make yourself comfortable. Find a cozy spot, pour yourself a cup of your favorite drink, and put your feet up. Let's spend a few moments together, and we'll tell you a little bit about ourselves and this can't-miss adventure broadly known as the Girlfriends' Getaway. It's an experience that will change your life. We know, because it has changed our lives. And every year it changes us again.

We are mother (Kathleen) and daughter (Elizabeth). But we're much more than that. We're also sisters and girlfriends. Confused? Hang in there. As we take you on this journey, you'll see what we mean. Stay with us because we have lots of surprises for you in this adventure, and we don't want you to miss any of them.

More than a decade ago, Kathleen and her mother and four sisters gathered for their first getaway. What began as a chance to reconnect, relax, and have some fun far away from family and work responsibilities turned into an annual event. Four years later Elizabeth and her cousin were invited to join in the adventure, and new traditions were formed. Since then the rest of the young women have also been included in the circle, boosting the number to thirteen.

Because our own adventure began with the five sisters, we call it our annual Sisters Weekend getaway. Another group calls theirs Laugh In, and a small band of women in Minnesota ride motorcycles on their adventure and call themselves The Hardly Angels. But no matter what you call your getaway or your group, the benefits are just as sweet. Would you believe us if we told you that enjoying a Girlfriends' Getaway on a regular basis could help you live longer? Or that it could enhance every area of your life—body, mind, and soul? We're telling you the honest truth.

It's just the girls here, so we can talk. When was the last time you took some time—even a brief moment—just for yourself? Think back to that time, no matter how long ago it was. Now, how did it make you feel? Did it feel really good, or did you feel a little guilty? Remember, we're being honest.

Now, recall another memory: the last time you laughed so hard that you doubled over and your sides hurt. When you were a kid, the experience of side-splitting laughter was a fairly common occurrence. It felt good to laugh, and it still does. But when was the last time you experienced such hilarity?

Here's what we're getting at. As a woman, you have a lot of people who depend on you. You spend most of your time meeting their needs but not much time meeting your own. Every now and then, you need to take some time off. You need to do something special for yourself. You need to gather with close friends. You need to relax and have fun, even laugh your head off. These things came naturally when you were a girl. They were great stress relievers back then, when life wasn't even all that stressful. How much more do you need these benefits today?

According to recent health statistics, women experience more fatigue than men, and it's no wonder. We work eighty-five hours per week between home and career. Almost 13 percent of us are divorced; 25 percent of us never even married. More than 17 percent of women are single moms, 29.9 percent of whom support their children on a poverty-level income. Overall, more women than men are likely to be poor. Even college-educated women, on average, earn fifteen thousand dollars per year less than their male counterparts.[1]

But while our pay scale still lags behind, our incidence of certain health problems is beginning to climb to the level formerly associated with men. In short, our overall health is deteriorating. We now rival men in the rate of heart disease, and the life span advantage we've enjoyed is declining. We could go on, but you get the point: The all-consuming pressures of relationships, career, and other responsibilities are taking their toll. We're being swept under by the current of daily life, but who's handing us a life vest? It appears that once again the solution is up to us.

Perhaps you don't want to hear that. After you've put in your weekly eighty-five hours, the thought of taking time for yourself is beyond ridiculous. No, it's not. It's necessary. As women, we take care of everyone else, why not ourselves? Self-care is a health requirement, not a selfish indulgence, and it's not reserved for the wealthy.

Dr. Michelle Battistini, director of the University of Pennsylvania's Penn Health for Women Center, identified what we should already know: "A lot of [health] complaints that women are bringing to me have some basis in the fact that they are just trying to do too much in too little time." In fact, when a group of doctors was asked what one thing women should do for their health, the answer was "take time for yourself."[2] By neglecting our own needs, we're making ourselves sick.

The good news is that we have discovered a health regimen that you're going to love. It doesn't involve getting up before sunrise for a daily three-mile jog. It doesn't require giving up chocolate in favor of fresh fruit and raw vegetables. And it doesn't even cost a lot of money. The health plan we recommend is as simple as spending time with other people you love, the women who are closest to you.

A Girlfriends' Getaway is a time to invest in yourself and in the lives of other women. It involves older women mentoring younger women and younger women enriching the lives of older women. It involves mothers and daughters and cousins and friends, high-school classmates, former college roommates, and friends from church, clubs, the office, or the neighborhood. It's about women of all ages and all walks of life coming together to enjoy one another, to relax, to be themselves, and to be renewed. It's an experience full of love and laughter and personal care that de-stresses, energizes, renews, and refreshes—if you do it right.

With a little advance planning, a Girlfriends' Getaway is as easy to pull off as a silk ribbon on a beautifully wrapped package. We promise to help you find the time to immerse yourself in the adventure that you and the special women in your life need.

PICTURE A GETAWAY

Imagine yourself and a few of your closest friends and sisters, or even a combination of both, enjoying some time away. What does it look like? Are you lying on a sunny beach watching the waves roll in or sitting in front of a crackling fire in a cozy cabin in the woods? Do you prefer the elegance of a high-rise hotel in the city or the pampering amenities of a health spa in a resort area? Or maybe it's a simple pajama party in the living room that pops into your mind.

Keep imagining the scene. Once you all get together, what happens? Do you hear laughter, quiet conversation, or singing? Are you playing games, hiking, watching a movie? The experience is yours to create. Girlfriends' Getaways can take as many different forms as there are women. It's not about where you are, how much money you spend, or even how long you're together. It's about your desire to invest in one another.

Come with us as we take a look at different groups of women who enjoy their own getaway adventures. They are women just like you, and they have discovered the joy of supportive sistering.

 bumps and bruises

WHAT TO EXPECT

As you start to imagine your own Girlfriends' Getaway, be careful about your expectations. If there's anything we've learned from getting together with a diverse group, it's to go with the flow. You can make all the plans you want, but when it comes down to your actual getaway, the goal should always be to enjoy your time and not get bogged down by big plans and expectations.

You can't schedule the perfect experience, so don't even try. You just have to let it unfold. We mention this early in the book because it's probably the top deterrent to a positive getaway experience. So remember to keep an open mind and be flexible. Sometimes the best aspect of the adventure isn't planned by anyone—it just happens!

The Birth of a Tradition

She was the last of the women to be picked up. She'd been pacing the driveway for some time, her eyes searching for their car, her bags lined up on the sidewalk like soldiers waiting for their orders. The energy had been mounting all morning, and now she was so excited she could hardly stand still. She'd played this scene over and over in her mind: the six of them talking, laughing, sharing together—without children, husbands, responsibilities of any kind. No demands, just fun!

She glanced at her watch again. If they didn't get here soon, she'd make a call to track them down. Just then, the sound of a car caught her ear. She began to jump up and down, unable to control her delight as she heard the squeals and calls of the other women. The car screeched to a stop, and four doors flew open. She was engulfed in hugs, kisses, and chatter—all the while being propelled toward the car.

Then a single voice rose above the noise. "You have got to be kidding. We will never get all that stuff in here!" Each head swiveled from the platoon of bags lined up on the pavement to the tiny space reserved for this last rider. Never underestimate determined women, however. With bags piled high, totes under toes, groceries on laps, knees drawn up to chins, and every square inch of space occupied, they headed off to start their adventure.

Did you guess where that story came from? Yes, it's a description of Kathleen's mother and sisters anxiously heading off on their very first Sisters Weekend. Kathleen says,

> The space we shared was ordinary by most standards, a simple
> hotel room. What made it extraordinary was that we shared it. We

managed to eat, sleep, shower, dress, and beautify ourselves while having longed-for conversations that were way overdue. We were free to be lighthearted, even crazy and silly, without having to be mom, wife, boss, or coworker. We didn't have to fulfill any role that demanded something of us.

We were thrilled to be together, but our weekend didn't just happen. In fact, we faced so many obstacles in planning that first getaway that it almost didn't happen. It meant leaving small children, taking time off from work, facing financial challenges, and for one of us, finding care for a disabled husband. But through commitment, determination, and careful planning, we all managed to free up the time, save up the money, make the necessary arrangements, and be there for one another.

In that little hotel room we began to appreciate one another in a new way. We discovered things about ourselves as sisters and friends that had never been revealed before or had been buried under years of adult responsibility. We fell in love again with our own family. It was intoxicating and freeing. Our lives took on whole new dimensions. We returned home different people, more joyful and confident, ready to invest ourselves in others with new vigor and a deepened commitment. We carried with us the positive energy we had gained from our concentrated time together.

It's not unique to us, this longing and need to spend meaningful time together, to connect and catch up with one another in a special time and place. Let's take a peek at another group of women who have found a unique way to celebrate one another.

A Celebration of Life

Eyes sparkle and roll with laughter as the women open the album, pull out the carefully preserved photo, and pass it around the table. "Unbelievable!" one of them says. "Whose idea was it to take this crazy picture?" Each year they admire this photograph, an image of the five of them showing off what they consider their best feature—the fabulous legs they inherited. They reminisce about the day the photo was taken. They had just come in from the beach and wanted to take one more photo of their annual gathering. At first, they stood in the traditional lineup pose they naturally fell into. That's when the youngest prompted, "C'mon, let's not be so boring! I have an idea." Now, years later, they stare again at the result and laugh at what they see—no bodies, no smiling faces, just a row of ten beautiful bare legs lined up like the Rockettes ready to start their kicks. The picture is sassy and lively, and it reveals something about these women. It shows they have a robust sense of humor and plenty of zest for life.

The women in this leggy photo, now laughing over the picture at their ocean-side retreat, are not showgirls. In fact, they're all grandmothers. But when they get together, they feel like teenagers. Each year they leave their Midwest farmland homes behind for this precious time in the Florida sunshine. It has grown into an unvarying tradition. They tell stories of "the old days," and they devote generous amounts of time to acting silly. For one weekend a year, they aren't respectable grandmothers; they're a small band of carefree adventurers who come together to affirm one another, to share their love, and to enjoy life.

The highlight of their annual gathering is the combined celebration of their birthdays, which they use to joyfully affirm their bond. Wearing colorful party hats and with arms linked, they encircle their cake, brilliant with candles. Swaying back and forth, their happy faces shining in the glow of birthday light, they serenade one another with favorite songs of celebration and merriment. "To life!" they cheer, and the party begins.

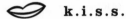 **k.i.s.s.**

Picture Perfect

Did you ever wonder why celebrities always look so good in photos? It's because they know how to pose. To help you capture the very best girlfriend photos for your getaway album, we'll let you in on a few of their secrets. You might feel silly trying some of these, but trust us, they work!

- Don't look at the camera straight on. Instead, tilt your head just a bit. You'll look more interesting—even a little exotic!
- Here's a modeling tip: Stand or sit slightly below the level of the camera. This limits your number of chins to just one.
- Turn a little to the side and lean ever so slightly forward. It makes you look thinner. Really!
- Take your pictures outside if possible—photos always look better in nature. But keep the subjects up close and watch that trees and branches don't "sprout" from someone's head. A great time for outdoor photos is right before sunset.
- If you want the entire group to get into the picture, use a tripod. You can buy tiny foldable ones that you can perch on any surface.
- Use a flash, even outside, to fill in the light.
- Avoid the standard "lineup." Instead, arrange everyone in a natural pose.
- Smile, smile, smile. You're having fun, so why not show it?

Going Deeper

The Girlfriends' Getaway adventure can range from the completely carefree to the deeper care of one another. It encompasses lifelong friends and newfound acquaintances. It includes those who have lost touch but now seek to regain a connection.

It's only recently that this type of bond has been forged among a group of thirteen women who met in high school and college. Tonight they sit cross-legged in a circle. In the tiny cabin, their youthful days of big dreams seem very far away. They listen carefully to every story that is shared. With such a large group, getting a chance to be heard can be difficult, so each one takes a turn. They relate the events that have shaped their lives and maybe even left a few emotional scars in the shaping process. It's late, but they're hesitant to break up the circle, so they continue talking into the morning.

They are traveling together on an important and sometimes difficult journey. This evening is not filled with laughter. They do smile from time to time, but most of the sharing has to do with dreams that failed to materialize, desires that remain unfulfilled, and fears that linger along the fringes of their lives. These stories are not easily told, but this is a safe place to lay their souls bare. They know they'll be cared for.

In the early years, filled with the optimism of youth, these friends used to gather simply to carouse and blow off steam. Those days were fun but were more about temporary enjoyment than about honest relationships. Back then their friendship was convenient. Today it's powerful. Back then self-centeredness and superficiality were the rule of the day. Now the challenges of marriages and careers, the deaths of loved ones, and the struggles associated with motherhood have brought them to a new truth: They need to be real, and they need the affirmation and support of one another.

"In the competitive world I live in, it sometimes seems as if women have forgotten the art of caring," one of the friends tearfully confides. "It's as if we don't know how to do it anymore. But getting together like this breaks down those barriers." They now see one another with eyes of empathy. They have begun to discover the depths of one another's souls. They have embarked on an adventure that will bring treasures they have long dreamed of but had almost given up on.

YOUR OWN GETAWAY

There you have it—three pictures of different types of Girlfriends' Getaways. Did you see yourself fitting into any of these scenes? Maybe so; maybe not completely. That's okay. This adventure is whatever you and your girlfriends create, not a formula that has to be followed. It takes on whatever shape you need. It doesn't have to be a weekend, and the women don't have to be related, come from the same age group, or even live near one another. You design the getaway to fit your lifestyle and your needs. If it's a reunion with high-school classmates, a gathering of actual sisters, or a cup of coffee poured between newfound soul mates, what matters is that you're doing it.

We'll drop in on additional Girlfriends' Getaway moments in the following chapters as we prepare you to launch your own adventure. And it truly is an adventure because it challenges you, changes you, exhilarates you, and helps you discover one of the most precious and valuable gifts of all: the strength that comes through intimate relationships.

You'll hear the word relationship a lot in this book, not only because it's the core concept but also because we've learned that, as women, we need to be in community to thrive. If we're not thriving, we're not fully living. And if we're not fully living, we can't be fully giving to the other people in our lives. Ericka McConnel, writing in *O* magazine, said it well:

> Women are natural comfort-givers—often to everyone but themselves. Why do so many of us run ourselves ragged trying to be the perfect wife, mother, friend, and worker? Perhaps because we have mistaken self-care for selfishness, and having denied our own needs, we don't know how to find help. The only way to extend comfort is to first open ourselves up to it. That means asking for the support we need—and believing that we are worthy of it. For when we know how to comfort ourselves, we can give to others not out of a sense of guilt but from our own strength."[3]

We firmly believe one of the best comforts in life is the company of close friends. Call them sisters, girlfriends, or soul mates, the meaning is the same. Throughout the following chapters, we'll show you how to draw from the riches of women who invest in one another. We'll help you discover how to thrive, not just survive.

FIELD NOTES

Chapter 2

DISCOVER YOUR GIRLFRIENDS

A GUIDE TO RECRUITING THE RIGHT WOMEN

A friend will mold a heroine out of a common woman. —BARBARA JENKINS

W e'd like you to meet Judy. She's a good friend who has listened to stories about various Girlfriends' Getaways for years and has tried to duplicate the experience with her two sisters. The three of them have rented hotel rooms for the weekend and sequestered themselves, trying to fulfill Judy's desire for them to become more than sisters—to become bona fide girlfriends.

The results have been less than encouraging. Nothing horrible—just not the life-changing, super-bonding, joyfully good time that Judy had hoped for. One of Judy's sisters seems to come to their weekends under duress and puts little or no effort into the getaway. It's as if she believes that since Judy extended the invitation (as she always does), it's Judy's job to pull the weekend together. Judy ends up taking care of all the logistics, as well as feeling responsible for everyone's having a good time. So at every getaway, Judy ends up creating unnecessary stress for herself when she could be relaxing and having fun.

Even worse, sibling rivalries sometimes flare up. Judy and her sisters get involved in petty spats over things such as what to have for dinner. A simple discussion about Chinese versus Mexican escalates into a "you-*always*-get-your-way" shouting match. And *shouting* isn't too strong a word for what happens. Exasperated by her failed attempts to pull off the weekend getaways that she had dreamed of, Judy keeps trying to figure out what she's doing wrong. We don't think it's a matter of *what* she's doing, but rather *with whom* she's doing it.

Girlfriends' Getaways work best when you invite the right girl-friends. Yes, we hear the collective "duh" on that one, but making up the invitation list may not be as simple as you think. Choosing the right girlfriends is essential to the success of your getaway, and it's worth it to devote a little time and careful thought to this decision. But don't panic. You can find just the right group of girlfriends to get your adventure started.

If you and your sisters enjoy one another's company, they might be the best friends to invite, especially if you desire a closer connection with them. If that's not a possibility, think beyond family bonds to other women in your life: old friends, new friends, cousins, your mother, even your grandmothers. This adventure is for anyone with whom you desire a closer, more honest, more supportive relationship. If you, like Judy, have tried getaways with the same group and failed to connect, it may be time to start over and invite another set of girlfriends. Now, it's time to start looking.

Where to Look

You may be unsure who your girlfriends really are. Are they your neighbors, your coworkers, your college buddies, or those women you just met last weekend? On the other hand, you may already be getting writer's cramp because your list of girlfriends is so long. You're struggling to decide who *not* to invite. In either case, we encourage you to read on. You'll find ideas in this chapter that will answer your questions, confirm your decision, and help you begin to plan an adventure you'll want to repeat year after year.

The success of a Girlfriends' Getaway doesn't depend on an exotic location, luxurious accommodations, or gourmet meals. The catalyst that produces a meaningful and life-changing experience is your group of girlfriends. Choosing the right women for the circle of sisterhood is the most important step in the process. And remember the definition of *sistering:* women coming alongside one another to supply strength where each one needs it.

Let's begin with an obvious, but essential, question: Who are the women in your life who have what it takes to meet this definition of sistering? There are as many right answers as there are women. But to narrow the field a bit, ask yourself: "Who are the women I feel closest to?" Don't limit your answer to women with whom you have family ties or a shared history or those who elicit a sense of obligation. It's not who you *should* feel closest to, but who you *are* closest to.

Think about the qualities of a close relationship. Who do you bare your soul to when you just can't hold your feelings inside any longer? Who do you trust with your secret hopes and dreams? If you don't have anyone in your life who fits that description, who would you like to have as that kind of friend?

Ideally, you have biological sisters. You've been around one another for your entire lives and already know one another inside and out. If you and your sisters have a relationship of trust and respect, recruit them for your adventure. We wish everyone were so fortunate, because one of the goals of this book is to help you strengthen family ties. But if you don't have sibling sisters, or if you and your sisters don't share a close relationship, then you'll need to look elsewhere. Your very best friends will become your sisters, and your family will grow to encompass them.

Sometimes a special relationship begins with a shared hobby or pastime that can develop into a treasured friendship. Are you in a club or social group with women whom you'd like to know on a deeper level? The Hardley Angels, whom we mentioned in chapter 1, are a perfect example of this. They began a relationship through their husbands' love of motorcycle riding. As these women spent their summer weekends on the road with the guys, they soon discovered their own affinity for "the bike" and the great outdoors. That's when the girls began their own weekday motorcycle jaunts into the countryside. Eventually the challenge of the ride—the wind blowing past their faces, the freedom of the road, the speed and power of the machines—developed into an admiration and respect for one another as strong, capable, and daring women.

"It's a wonderful feeling riding in the fresh air—kind of taking a risk—smiling at your girlfriends after a great run on a curvy road. The camaraderie is something else," says one of The Hardly Angels. We love the adventurous spirits of these women. Recently they began another chapter in their quest to spend more time together riding and, at the same time, to know one another more deeply. They've found that these relational experiences are filled with surprises and challenges, much like their open-road escapades. But the rewards are infinitely more precious.

As we indicated earlier, we can help you find girlfriends in the most unusual places, even on a Harley. These angels in leather prove that sometimes girlfriends come together under the auspices of a shared hobby or passion and only later discover that they also share the bond of being true girlfriends. Maybe you, too, have a group that shares the same hobby or recreational interest. If so, draw from this group to find your potential getaway mates. If you're still stumped, then you're just a hopeless case.

Kidding, kidding—we're just kidding. Read on, and get more inspiration. We promise that by the time you finish the chapter, you'll have a list of names of girlfriends you can't wait to bring together.

THOSE WHO DON'T QUALIFY

Warning! As you draw up your list of girlfriends, be aware of who *not* to include. For example, don't invite your boss or certain coworkers (you know which ones) or anyone you may feel obligated to invite. (Girlfriends' Getaway is not about obligation!) Also, if you have ulterior motives in inviting a person—to impress her or to win favor—then you're looking in the wrong place. A Girlfriends' Getaway has nothing to do with getting ahead in your career or currying favor with influential women in your social circle.

If you ignore this very important piece of advice, all we can say is that you were warned. Not only will you be shortchanging yourself of true friendships that may well last a lifetime, but your getaway will be awkward and more work than play. You'll wear yourself out in no time chasing an unattainable goal that, in the end, won't benefit you or your invited girlfriends. If you really want to impress someone, organize a brunch, host a benefit, marry a millionaire. (Again—just kidding. We

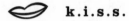 **k.i.s.s.**

AN IRRESISTIBLE INVITATION

Personalized invitations are a great way to set a tone and get everyone excited about the upcoming event. You can buy standard invitations if you want. But if you're feeling adventurous, go ahead and create your own distinctive cards. Here are easy ways to do that:

- Cut up inexpensive geological survey maps into invitation cards. This gives the getaway an adventure/travel theme. (You can usually find these maps at sporting goods stores that carry outdoor equipment.)
- Buy flower seed packets and enclose them in your invitation along with the message, "Come along as we plant the seeds of true sisterhood."
- Send each girlfriend a box containing the ingredients for a clay mask to be used for a facial during the getaway. Many health food stores sell single-serving dry masks in their own envelopes. On the invitation mention that "we'll be taking off our masks." You could also drop a

hope you're catching on to our sense of humor.) The point is to protect your getaway adventures for your true girlfriends and *no one else*.

Now, how's that list coming along? Got a few names, don't you? Good! The list you come up with deserves a lot of thought, because it will determine the nature and ultimate success of your getaway. We know we've said that a few times now, but it's because we so strongly want you to have the best getaway possible. Without the right

---

hint about the spa day you'll have, and tell your girlfriends to bring their "invitations" along. (For more ideas on a do-it-yourself day spa, see appendix 3.)

- If you're hosting the getaway in your city, use postcards of local points of interest or a place you know you'll be visiting, and tell your girlfriends, "There's more to come!"

- Raid your local art supply store or paper store and purchase beautiful handmade paper. Look for stickers bearing quotes from famous women to use on your handmade invitations. Or you can script your own!

- Find an old picture of all of you—maybe even from high school or junior high—and photocopy it on a good copier or use your card-making software. Make it the cover for your invitations.

- Check with your library or bookstore for books geared to children's parties—they often have the best ideas for invitations.

---

girlfriends, you'll likely find yourself having a Mere Acquaintances Getaway, a Nearly Strangers Getaway, or, worse, an Enemies Getaway! Who wants to put all this effort into an experience that's doomed from the start? So now that we've driven that point home, let's look at a few different types of girlfriends and consider how to get them fired up for your getaway adventure.

OUT-OF-TOUCH GIRLFRIENDS

If you have sisters or good friends but have lost touch with them, you might feel awkward about inviting them to a getaway right out of the blue. But awkward or not, you know what you've got to do: Pick up that phone, girl! Send that e-mail! Write that letter! So what if you haven't talked in a while? If you're missing them, they're probably missing you, too. What's the worst that could happen? Your invitation *could* be rejected, so think about how you'd feel and then be prepared for it. It probably won't happen, but in your relief, you'll forget any anxiety you may have had, and you'll dash headlong into planning your first Girlfriends' Getaway.

FARAWAY GIRLFRIENDS

If your list of closest friends dates back to high school or college, it's likely that you are now a far-flung group. So how do you approach faraway friends? Actually, if you're separated by geographical distance, then a Girlfriends' Getaway is perfect for you. That's the case with our own group. Some of us live in one Midwestern state, while the others live several hundred miles away. But that's what makes our annual weekend so special, since it's the only time during the year that we're all together. We simply have to make a bit more of an effort to pull it off, and that's how it will be for you.

Don't let distance be a deterrent. In fact, let it keep you motivated so that you don't let anything get in the way of your precious time together. And all the catching up you'll be able to do on your shared adventure just might cut down on your long-distance bill.

On a practical note, you really can overcome distance, and you don't have to be independently wealthy to do it. Several of the Girlfriends' Getaway veterans we interviewed are scattered across the country, but they use that distance to their advantage. They alternate visiting one another's home cities, or they meet at a central location and explore a place where they've never been. Since their getaway is held only once a year, they have plenty of time to plan and save money.

If you or any of your girlfriends will be traveling by plane, be sure to plan the adventure as early as possible. That way, you have a greater chance of getting a good deal on airfare. Better yet, shop around in cyberspace for a low fare. Booking travel on-line is fast and easy and can save you money. You'll often find great deals, regularly updated, on the Internet. Check the Web sites of several major airlines a number of times over a few weeks to find the best deals. If you've never booked on-line before, think of this as part of your new adventure!

GIRLFRIENDS WHO NEED COAXING

When you first approach a friend with the idea of a getaway adventure, she may be resistant. She may even say that she'd rather not participate. What should you do if that happens?

Remember Judy? She invited her sisters for a weekend adventure, and things didn't pan out. Initially, the women she invited weren't convinced that this was really for them. If that's what you encounter when you start inviting women to join you, handle the situation delicately.

You don't want to force anyone into spending time with you, even though you know that she'd have a wonderful time *and* she really doesn't know what she's missing *and* she's *crazy* to decline this fabulous opportunity *and*...! Okay, let's take a breath and think this one through. Why is she opposed to the idea? Did you have a fight? If so, apologize, whether you think it was your fault or not. Has your relationship drifted? Well, a Girlfriends' Getaway is the perfect way to remedy that, but your friend may not know that—yet. Why not send her a copy of this book? Use it as the tool it is, and let it speak for you.

Be patient. You can't force a friend to do something she doesn't want to do, much as you may like to. Do you really want to drag her along, kicking and screaming, just to prove that you were right? We didn't think so. For now you'll have to be the adult and let your friend decide for herself. It could be that she really doesn't care to invest in this type of relationship, and if that's the case, it's better not to force the issue.

In the meantime, try to foster a relationship. Go out with her for coffee or invite her to lunch. If she lives too far away to do that, give her a call once in a while and don't even mention the Girlfriends' Getaway. Extend friendship, not to pester her, but to show you care. Chances are, after she hears stories about your first getaway—which she missed—she'll soften up and agree to give it a try the following year. For now, organize an adventure with the rest of your girlfriends and have faith that some day your resistant sister will come around.

GIRLFRIENDS WITH LOGISTICAL CHALLENGES

A Girlfriends' Getaway sounds great in theory, but what about the very real challenges you'll face in trying to pull one off? For instance, if your girlfriend is a single mom, she probably lives on an extra-tight budget. Plus, it may be tough for her to find child care for the weekend. How can she possibly get away?

Girl, are we glad you asked! Single moms, perhaps more than anyone, need a Girlfriends' Getaway, and sadly they're often the last ones to get it. The spiritual restoration they receive from being with their closest friends, the balance that is restored to their lives, and the support they feel from such a group brings them back to their children a stronger and more optimistic mom.

We're going to change the tone for a moment so we can show you a group of single moms who've begun their own very special getaway time. Looking at these six women seated around a large dining room table pouring tea for one another, we could easily mistake them for royalty. "One lump or two?" asks one. "Milk or lemon?" asks another. The fine china barely emits a clink as they set their cups down to reach for delicate scones. Enveloped in this moment, some of them are surprised that their thoughts rarely focus on home and children. They are present in the moment, enjoying the chance to momentarily escape their routines and relish the richness of time with friends.

It has taken determination and a special commitment just to be here. Rather than go away for an entire weekend, they've decided to gather at one woman's home for a leisurely afternoon. Although less of a burden on their wallets, it's still a sacrifice of time and energy. It's difficult to make the commitment to break away from their responsibilities as single moms.

But now they can relax in the company of girlfriends. As the afternoon progresses, they enter a world of lighthearted joy. The warmth of the tea they sip is a comfort, and they settle into a rhythm of happy conversation. Not a word about work, kids, or daily stresses is spoken. This is their time to escape.

An hour ago the scene was very different. The cares several of these friends brought from home were released in tears as they shared some of their biggest concerns.

"I almost didn't make it here today; I have so much on my mind," one mom confided. "It seemed selfish to come. After all, this is the only time all week that I have alone with my kids. But I also need a break sometimes. I need to be with women like you who understand and who can help me laugh at my life. Getting away like this is something I just have to do once in a while."

"I know what you mean," said another woman. "I've been single for a lot longer than most of you, and I've managed pretty well most of the time if I do say so myself." She chuckled. "But raising two teenagers alone is taking its toll on me. Making time for friends, even for a little while, is turning out to be just what I need to feel like myself again."

The others nodded with looks of understanding.

Now, an hour later, as a fresh pot of tea is brought to the table, they lift their china cups for lingering sips of the fragrant, steaming brew. They laugh at one another's stories and share hopes and dreams for the future. And before the afternoon ends, they make plans for another special girlfriends' escape.

This is a true story, not one we cooked up for purposes of illustration. In this group of single women, not one of the girlfriends regretted having to arrange an afternoon away from her kids. Yes, it was hard at first; yes, it was a sacrifice; and yes, it was worth every minute.

We strongly encourage you to include your single friend, even if she can join the group only for a day or a few hours. Help her with child care if you can, either financially or physically, and be sensitive to her unique needs and possible objections: finances, time off from work, transportation, other tricky arrangements.

If *you* are a single mom, start the process by telling your friends what you want to do. They may be so glad to get some time with you that they'll do whatever it takes to make it happen. Start small—a couple of hours at a coffee shop or dessert at your place after the kids are in bed—and after you're comfortable with that, try something a little more elaborate.

The bottom line when inviting a single friend who has kids is this: No one can (or should) force her to go. It will take some extra effort to pull it off, but she *can* do it. Tell her exactly what you know about her: "Look at you, raising children on your own, doing the job of five people but without any of the glory, and doing it well. You've already achieved heroine status. Obviously, you can do anything you put your mind to, and a Girlfriends' Getaway is no different. The rewards will be immeasurable—far beyond the couple of hours or couple of days that you'll spend away from your children, and you'll be a better mom for it, too." Tell her that this will be a time of pure relaxation, bonding, and a chance to recharge those ultra long-life batteries she's been running on.

Competition for Your Time

We've spent all this time talking about the objections you may get from your girlfriends, but what about the hesitation *you* may be feeling? We know that you've got a lot on your plate already. For example, how many people depend on you? Too many to count on one hand—or even both hands (and both feet), right? So it's easy to wonder if a Girlfriends' Getaway is really the best use of your time. If you're married, you may be thinking it would be better to spend that time with your husband and kids. Or if you're single, you may not want to give up the time you usually spend with friends or with Mom and Dad or with your real best friend, Fluffy the cat. You could be asking yourself, *Shouldn't my family come first?*

There is another great question, and one that can be answered in much the same way as the question about single moms. Our families depend on us, and time with them is very important. But time to step away and renew ourselves is just as important. Yes, it's true—we have permission to take time for ourselves! Getting away with our sisters doesn't just benefit us. It spills over to benefit our families and friends as well. That time away makes us stronger and better able to be the kind of women we truly desire to be, whether we're married or single and whether we have children with two legs or four.

Both of us are married, and our husbands will tell you that our annual weekend spent with our circle of sisters is the best thing to come along since Monday Night Football. And it's not because they love to get us out of the house! They love it because they know how much *we* love it. Not only that, they see the difference in us—it makes us better wives and better mothers. One of the greatest gifts you can give your family is this time of personal renewal and discovery. If we could put a money-back guarantee on it, we would. You can make excuses until the proverbial cows come home, but our answers to your objections are summed up in the words of one of the women we interviewed for this book: "We make the commitment to spend time together. Other people, other things in our lives have to give way to it." As hard as it may be to get away, as busy as you are (aren't we all?), as financially strapped as you may be, the sacrifices you'll make can't compare to the benefits you'll receive.

In fact, our own Sisters Weekend group has faced just about all of these limitations, and yet without exception we have come together every year since 1990. During these years, one of us had the responsibility of caring for a chronically ill husband, several of us had small children to leave with dads, a few of us lived long distances from the others, some of us had to overcome financial limitations, one of us was a single working mom, and all of us at one time or another had career or school responsibilities. There's no magic formula to making this work. What it takes is simple determination fueled by the knowledge that there is nothing in our lives quite like spending time with the circle of sisters.

As long as we're setting the example here, we'll let you in on a little secret: We don't always make it to every one of our Sisters Weekends. Yes, it's true—at times one or two of us have had to skip a year because the limitations described above were just too great. We're telling you this so that you won't get discouraged if one of your girlfriends can't make it or be dogmatic in saying that "we all go or we don't go at all." Keep in mind the big picture, which is an ongoing getaway with your girlfriends that you can count on for the refreshment and support you need. We don't want to paint you a false picture or build you an icon of unattainable perfection. What we *do* want is to help you lay the foundation for a wonderful time that is unlike any other in your life. We're not perfect, but we keep on going, growing, and strengthening our commitment to our Girlfriends' Getaway.

The Perfect Number of Girlfriends

Speaking of perfection, there is one way we can help you get quite close to it: Decide how many women to invite. As mundane as this may sound, you will thank us later for bringing it up. We learned on our first weekend adventure that six women in one hotel room (read: two beds, two roll-aways, one bathroom) is far from ideal. Sure you may live to tell about it, as we did, or—banish the thought—you all get too close for comfort and swear you'll never step foot in the same room again. That's why you need to think now about where you may spend your first Girlfriends' Getaway and how many of you that place can accommodate.

Take our group of sisters, for example. There are now thirteen of us, so we know we need a large place, such as a condo or townhouse or large cabin. Luckily, with that many people sharing the cost, we can afford it. Finding the perfect number of friends, however, can be tricky, so you'll need to do some research to find a place that is large enough so you can all breathe but small enough so you don't have to spend a fortune to stay there. (We'll talk more about that in the following chapter.)

One more piece of advice: If you have your heart set on going to one particular location and you know that you can only get a hotel room there, limit your list of girlfriends. (You may be tempted to simply get multiple rooms, but we hesitate to recommend that for a couple of reasons. First, your group may end up splintered into two groups of roommates. Second, you know that the best conversations take place in the wee hours, and if you're not all in the same place, it's just not the same.) If you have more latitude, say a choice between a cabin or a condo, feel free to expand the list and find a place that will accommodate a larger group.

Before we go on, we want to commend you for taking the initiative to set yourself and your closest friends on a journey that will lead to joy and fulfillment, not to mention fun. Now that you've taken the first step, don't give up. You'll soon be surrounded and lifted up by your circle of sisters, and believe us, there's nothing like it. Not even chocolate.

Now, grab that phone and start dialing!

FIELD NOTES

Chapter 3

SET UP CAMP

CHOOSE THE PLACE THAT'S RIGHT FOR YOU

There are no shortcuts to any place worth going. — BEVERLY SILLS

If recruiting the right girlfriends is the most important step in pulling off a successful getaway, choosing the right place ranks a very close second. Finding the location that fits the needs and personality of your circle of sisters makes all the difference. Likewise, choosing a place that is ill-suited, for whatever reason, just about guarantees frustration and, in our experience, a few tears.

Let us tell you a story that's mildly disturbing. It's mostly true, but certain details have been altered to protect the guilty.

Once upon a time, there was a circle of sisters who couldn't wait to arrive at the cabin they had rented for their weekend adventure. They'd never had an entire cabin just to themselves. In past getaways they had shared a crowded hotel room, but this year they'd have plenty of space to stretch out. The sisters had visions of cooking scrumptious meals in the kitchen, lounging in the ample living room, drinking their morning coffee on the deck, and talking until all hours in front of a cozy fire in the grand stone fireplace.

The day finally arrived, and they drove up to what would be their home for the next three days. All eyes gazed upward at the delightful sight they beheld—a lovely structure situated nicely on top of a hill, with prairie all around and not a soul for miles. Well, okay, they had thought it would be nestled in the woods, not stranded in the middle of a field. But these sisters were old hands at weekend getaways. Woods or field, it didn't really matter. Their joy at being together crowded out any momentary disappointment, so they quickly unpacked the car and made their way up the hill. The climb was a little steeper than it looked, and they hoped they'd remembered to bring everything. It wasn't a hike they wanted to repeat anytime soon.

When they reached the top, the oldest member of the group unlocked the door. What wonders would they behold in this charming cabin? They could hardly contain their excitement. Then the door swung open, and the simultaneous, audible gasp of six women who were *completely taken aback* rolled out across the open prairie. A long moment of silence followed, until finally one of them spoke up: "Well, it's bigger than the hotel room all right!"

No outward response came from the rest. But in the silence, they were all thinking, and thinking hard. They had dreamed of a quaint cabin that would exude warmth and homeyness and comfort. But this dusty building was old and run down. No, that's being kind. It was downright depressing.

Not to fear—these women were veterans of the annual getaway adventure. Something as minor as a dirty, broken-down old cabin sitting in the middle of an open field wasn't going to get them down. Bags in hand, they charged inside and began claiming the space as their own.

As they unpacked, the sister who had reserved the cabin began to explore. As she did, her brow became more and more furrowed, her frown became deeper, and the tears nearly blurred her vision—which was probably a blessing, because she really didn't want to see any more of this place. She discovered a kitchen that could only accommodate half a person and a microwave that couldn't hold even a bag of popcorn. She sat on one of the cabin's two beds, and it nearly sagged to the floor. The water in the bathroom ran brownish, and the shower either scalded or froze its miserable occupant. *Why didn't I inspect this place before I booked it?* she wondered. As she mentally kicked herself, she was convinced that the weekend would be ruined and it was all her fault.

She nearly slumped to the floor and gave in to the tears that had been threatening to roll down her cheeks. But before she admitted defeat, her ears perked up. What was that sound? It almost sounded like…yes, it was laughter. Where could it be coming from in *this* dreary place? She peeked around the corner. Her sisters had found the one spot that lived up to their expectations, and they were enjoying it to the fullest. There on the deck, that huge deck that the saddened sister had read about, was a table spread with a bounty of hors d'oeuvres and refreshments. Her lovely sisters were there, laughing louder than she'd heard them laugh in a long time. She breathed a sigh of relief as a smile crept across her face, and she hurried to join the celebration.

This story, thankfully, has a happy ending, but it could just as easily have turned into a three-day nightmare. The difference, of course, was in everyone's attitude. But if it hadn't been for the spacious deck, even a good attitude might not have triumphed over that "cozy cabin in the woods." Which brings us back to rule number two: *Find the right accommodations.* Because we've been through it all before, we're going to make sure that you don't end up with a story similar to the one above.

Stay Inside the Box

Normally, we wouldn't tell you to stay in your comfort zone, but when it comes to overnight accommodations, that's exactly what you should do. Do you and your girlfriends like to camp? One group of women who love the outdoors began their getaways by hiring someone to guide them on a weekend mountain trek. Maybe something rustic will fit the bill for you, too. Or are you like one of our sisters whose idea of camping is ordering room service? If so, don't book a place in the hinterlands. Instead, consider splurging on a room at the fanciest hotel you can find, or even a nice condo on the beach. If there are several of you, you can probably afford it and be comfortable, too. The general rule to follow is this: Analyze your collective vacation personalities and go from there.

We know one group of old friends from high school who are scattered all over the country. Each year they take turns hosting the others in their home city. They all enjoy city life, so they take advantage of what big cities have to offer: great theater, dining, clubs, and shopping.

They know what they like to do together and where they're most comfortable doing it—and they do it well.

 bumps and bruises

WHERE TO SLEEP

Head off potential lodging conflicts right away by deciding beforehand who will get the "nice room." If you're staying at a condo or other multiroom lodging, there's always a nice room that is supposed to be the master suite. Who gets it? Here are a few possible solutions:

- If one person really wants it, she can pay a little more than the others.
- Share it—let a different person have it on a rotating basis.
- Flip for it, and no complaints allowed!

You may come up with better alternatives. The point is to be aware of it before you arrive so you won't be walking into conflict right away.

CONSIDER THE COST

Whatever type of lodging you decide on, remember to factor in the price. If you're all millionaires, then skip this paragraph. For the rest of you, keep in mind the girlfriend who probably has the least amount of money to spare, then keep your prices at that level. If you have a large group, you'll find that you can afford fairly lavish accommodations by splitting the cost.

For example, this year our group is going to a resort where we'll rent a condo that has several bedrooms, two kitchens, several bathrooms, and a hot tub. Sound extravagant? For three nights, we are each paying one hundred and fifty dollars! Of course, that doesn't include food and transportation, but we're not going too far, and we all take turns cooking so we only go out for one meal. This arrangement makes for a very comfortable and fun weekend adventure that's budget-friendly at the same time. If one hundred and fifty dollars sounds like a lot, you may find that "camping" at a girlfriend's home is the perfect solution. Slumber parties aren't just for junior-high kids anymore!

A group of women in Colorado stays at one woman's ranch home each year. They take turns cooking meals so that the hostess doesn't carry the entire burden. They greet the morning sun with exercise, they pray, and they talk into the wee hours—all of which cost nothing. (We bet you can afford nothing!) Not only are they having a great time on the cheap, but they've discovered something that truly refreshes their

 bumps and bruises

KEEP THINGS TIDY

Once you've selected your "camp," whether spacious or cozy, keep in mind that when more than one person is sharing a bedroom, bathroom, and other spaces, you need to keep clutter to a minimum. Be considerate of your girlfriends and use any drawers and closets that are available to put your things out of sight. It's easy to overpack and end up with a beautiful vacation rental that looks like it's been hit by a hurricane. That can spoil any getaway fast!

souls. For them, it's not even about how much or how little money they're spending; it's about doing something that they truly love, and that's a real treasure.

Chances are, however, that you'll be spending *something* on your getaway, and it's actually not as hard as you might think to save up whatever amount you'll need. (That's right, we're even going to tell you how to save money—what are girlfriends for?) Several years ago, one of our artistically inclined sisters made each of us a "saving jar." She bought blue antique pickle jars and painted a lake scene on each one, with the words "Sisters Weekend" and each person's name. Not only are they adorable, but they're practical, too. We keep them in plain sight, usually in our bedrooms or offices, to remind us to put a little something in them each week or month. One of us (not Kathleen, by the way) admits that she's not much of a saver, so having this visual reminder is wonderful!

A financial expert once made a suggestion for simple saving: Pay for everything with paper bills and each day put all of your change in a jar. In a month, you should have at least thirty dollars, money you probably never missed. Another strategy is to figure out your total outlay for the getaway, check how many months you have between now and then, and divide the former by the latter. Now you have a monthly amount (hopefully a modest one) that you can work into your budget. If a monthly sum seems high, break it down into weeks or days. Do you need three hundred and sixty dollars for your getaway next year? That's a dollar a day—no sweat!

Take our Sisters Weekend, for example. Our basic cost is one hundred fifty dollars, a figure that covers each person's lodging. We know at least nine months ahead of time how much the following year's adventure is going to cost, including food and transportation, so we divide the total by nine. Since we travel by car and cook for ourselves, it comes out to less than twenty-five dollars a month.

Another way to save the money ahead of time is to consider giving up a bad habit. One of our sisters gave up smoking and put her former cigarette money into her saving jar. She had her getaway budget set aside in no time and kicked a bad habit, too! Didn't we tell you a Girlfriends' Getaway would make you healthier?

THE VALUE OF SIMPLICITY

Since your getaway is not about sightseeing and touring, we don't recommend that you go to Disney World or the Grand Canyon or New York City. Of course, a little shopping and sightseeing is always fun, but if you find that is all you're doing, it's time to reevaluate. Your getaway will quickly get eaten up, and you may find yourselves at the end of the weekend having learned nothing more about one another than which one of you likes to cut in line. Even the high-school friends we mentioned who meet in big cities for their getaways are careful to make their relationships the top priority. One of these friends got it right: "We all really like each other and miss being around each other. It's great to have that one weekend a year to just be 'us' again, no responsibilities, no kids to chase, no husband to explain my nutty behavior to."

We encourage you to choose a place for your getaway that will allow plenty of time for relaxation. For example, our group likes to go to the shore of Lake Superior in northern Minnesota. Most of us live in Minnesota, and the North Shore is a beautiful area. We enjoy taking walks along the lakeshore and then sitting by the fireplace, on the deck, or in the whirlpool. Do you notice a pattern here? Our style is to do a lot of talking and sitting and sitting and talking. It's a luxury we enjoy this one weekend a year. When we're home, who has the luxury of just sitting and talking?

You've taken care to plan who will be at your getaway and where it will be, so once you get there, relax and allow the time you share to take on a life of its own. Calendars, deadlines, laptops, and pagers are left at home. (This is not merely a polite suggestion; it's a requirement.) Downtime, sharing, listening, relaxing, resting, and renewal should be uppermost on the getaway to-do list. To help simplify things, consider staying relatively close to home, especially for your first getaway. You want the focus to be on all of you, not your surroundings. Look for appropriate lodging within a four-hour driving radius. Not only does a nearby destination make for relatively familiar territory, it also dramatically reduces travel expenses. Go much more than a day's drive away and you'll be tempted to fly and add a few hundred dollars to your costs. So stay closer to home and use the extra money for gourmet food or nicer accommodations.

One more reason to steer clear of air travel is that it limits what you can bring with you. If you drive to your destination, you can bring plenty of food for easy, fun meals. You can also bring small gifts for everyone, your own music to share, games, books, and even costumes— if you and your girlfriends have a flair for the dramatic. So make it easy on yourself and don't travel too far.

That is, unless you and your sisters have always dreamed of a weekend of Broadway shows or seeing the sights in San Francisco. (Call us anything you want, but don't accuse us of being dogmatic.) If you can afford it, and a sightseeing vacation *doesn't get in the way of your quality time together,* then go for it. We know two sisters who plan a vacation in exotic places every year. They enjoy exploring together, and they have discovered much about each other through their adventures. So how do they keep these trips simple? By planning ahead, keeping it just between the two of them, going only where they want to go, and doing what they want to do. Sounds perfectly simple to us!

HOMEBOUND

This brings us to another situation you may find yourself in, as we did one year: You may not be able to go away at all. In our situation, a family member who needed care kept us homebound. Your situation may be family-related, or it could be financial limitations or time constraints that cause you to consider a homemade gathering. Whatever the case, don't despair. We used that situation as an opportunity to gather our sisters close to home, and we had our weekend adventure at Kathleen's mom's. She lives in a beautiful house on a lake, so it wasn't too much of a sacrifice. In fact, it turned out to be one of our most enjoyable weekends ever. We took the money we'd saved on accommodations and hired a nail technician to come to the house and give everyone manicures and pedicures. And we still managed to unwind with fun antics such as dancing the hula on the beach at night and slowing down time by cruising the lake during the day. It was wonderful!

In fact, you may choose to stay home simply because that's what appeals to you most. Staying home saves money, it's convenient, and it keeps you in familiar surroundings. One word of advice, however: If possible, stay with a girlfriend who lives alone. There's nothing refreshing about being interrupted by roommates, husbands, or children!

And as always, be creative. Plan some things that might normally seem extravagant. It doesn't have to be financially extravagant, either. To really refresh you, body and soul, we'll help you turn your home into a day spa (see appendix 3). And for one of the most elegant and fun evenings imaginable, we recommend Hoity-Toity Night (see appendix 2). All we'll say here is bring your feather boas, long white gloves, and a little attitude.

If costumes and props don't fit your group, it's hard to beat a leisurely two-hour walk through your neighborhood or local park, stopping along the way to smell the roses. This simple exercise may actually seem quite extravagant compared to what you normally have the time or energy to do. You don't live in a quiet, leafy neighborhood? How about a big pot of coffee, a couple of really fattening scones (we're still talking extravagant), and enough conversation to finish them off? We can provide all kinds of suggestions, but you get the idea. Only you know the kinds of activities that will really make you feel restored, and we'll say it again—get creative!

Check Out Your Destination

Here's a checklist to help you settle on a place to stay that will meet your group's needs. It's not an exhaustive list, but it's a good starting point to help you think of the things that will brighten your adventure.

- ❏ Is it clean? (You might be surprised at how many places aren't.)
- ❏ Is it spacious—how many beds and bathrooms?
- ❏ Does it have a kitchen—microwave, utensils, icemaker?
- ❏ Does it have a television, VCR, or stereo?
- ❏ Does it have a fireplace?

- ❏ Is there a pool or hot tub?
- ❏ Are there nearby attractions and restaurants?
- ❏ Is there a grocery store nearby?
- ❏ Is it easily accessible? Is there a freeway nearby or a major airport? Is it off the beaten path?
- ❏ What are the surroundings like? (Is it on a lake or ocean? Is it in the woods?)
- ❏ If you're booking a hotel room, be sure to ask:
  - What kind of view does the room have? (Many simply face other rooms.)
  - Does the room have corridor access or exterior access?
  - What kind of transportation is available from the airport (if you're flying in)?
  - What kind of restaurants are in the hotel and do they have 24-hour room service?
  - Do you need a car to get from the hotel to shopping, restaurants, and so forth?
  - Is there a refrigerator in the room (so you can keep cold drinks on hand)?
  - Is the hotel under any construction? (You'd be surprised how many wake up their guests at 6 A.M. with jackhammers.)

Use the space below to add your own needs, preferences, and requests:

....

....

....

Once you've narrowed down your choices, pay a visit to check the place(s) out firsthand. We hope the story at the beginning of this chapter speaks for itself on this point. Don't take the reservation agent's word for it, and don't trust the brochures. Speaking of which, read brochures carefully. Descriptions such as *cozy* could mean tiny; *rustic* might mean dilapidated or lacking indoor plumbing; *secluded* might even be out of range for a sled dog. When you go, bring along a friend who will catch things you might miss, both good and bad. You want to be aware not only of things that could hinder your enjoyment but also of things that will enhance your experience. Visiting potential getaway spots in person could make your decision much easier, especially if you're torn between two places. And don't forget to take along your checklist!

So you've chosen the place? Great! Sit down and pat yourself on the back. Well, that might be difficult, so pat yourself on the back first, then sit down. But before you get too comfortable, did you make the reservation? If not, grab the phone and reserve the place! Few things are more disappointing than locating your fantasy accommodations only to discover there's no vacancy for the next three years.

Okay, you've got it reserved? Now take a deep breath. You're well on your way to enjoying a Girlfriends' Getaway that will change your life.

FIELD NOTES

PART II | GET PACKING

Chapter 4

FOLLOW THE map

DIRECTIONS FOR A GREAT GETAWAY

Friends are treasures. — HORACE BRUNS

Remember *The Goonies,* a movie about a group of kids who found a map that led them on a great adventure? They discovered a pirate ship and ultimately the pirates' treasure. The challenges and dangers of following the map, the surprises and wonders of their experiences with the pirates, as well as the camaraderie of these friends made for an enjoyable tale for kids and adults alike.

In the spirit of those young adventurers, here is your very own treasure map. The goal of the journey is clear: precious time spent with your chosen goonies, er, girlfriends. And the route that will get you there has already been scouted by previous travelers. Now that you have a goal and a direction, you'll welcome the surprises along the way as part of the adventure.

The imagery of a treasure map is intentional. There is great treasure to be found on a Girlfriends' Getaway. After more than a decade of our own weekend adventures, we find that we value most the riches of fun—the refreshment and the de-stressing—and also the honest relationships that support and strengthen us. The treasure you find will be what you make it and what you need it to be.

To help you find the treasure while avoiding detours and wrong turns, this map includes checklists and other idea starters to help your getaway hit the ground running. It also includes some great ideas for things to do on your getaway. (Make sure you add your own ideas to these lists.) We've also included a sample itinerary adapted from one of our own Sisters Weekends. Finally, to make sure that you're really part of the circle of girlfriends, we've included an official oath of initiation. When you get to it, you'll find complete instructions for the induction ceremony. And yes, you have to do it!

WHAT TO BRING

If you're like a lot of women, the worst part of getting away is packing for the trip. The whole experience is fraught with indecision and "what ifs." You don't want to reach your destination only to discover that you don't have your favorite sweater or your toothbrush or (gasp!) your makeup. This has been the bane of the traveler's existence since time immemorial—until now. (Can you hear the dramatic music in the background? Cue resonant masculine voice.) We have assembled for you the most complete, most comprehensive packing list. Ever.

Okay, enough goofiness. You want helpful pointers. So here you go, our famous packing checklist. Feel free to add to it as you think of specific things that are unique to you and your getaway. The items are not necessarily listed in order of importance:

❑ bathing suit and beach towel

❑ sunscreen and self-tanner (See "Your Time in the Sun" in appendix 3.)

❑ pajamas and lightweight robe that could also double as a beach coverup (Bring a cute robe if you're doing a spa night. See appendix 3.)

❑ shampoo, if you're the designated shampoo-bringer for your group

❑ hair dryer and curling iron, if you're the designated bathroom-appliances-bringer

❑ necessary medications

❑ all ingredients for the meal you'll be in charge of:

....

....

....

....

....

....

❑ music and videos

❑ a portable CD player (Perhaps one person could bring this item so you don't end up with dueling CD players.)

❏ cameras—still and video (To save some space, you might consider designating one or two people to bring these items and have them be the official group photographer or videographer.)

k.i.s.s.

LIGHTEN YOUR LUGGAGE

Packing can be a dream or a nightmare, depending on how you go about it. We've learned from many years of annual getaways, and one of us is a former flight attendant—a professional packer of sorts. So before you throw every article of clothing you own into the largest suitcase you can find, remember these simple tips:

- Instead of folding your clothes, roll them. Not only will you fit more into your luggage, but you'll get fewer wrinkles.

- Wrap your clothes in the plastic that covers your dry cleaning. Your clothes will slide around more easily and won't rub against each other, which causes wrinkles.

- Use the layered look. Pack a twin set or T-shirt and a light sweater or shawl instead of one heavy sweater. You get double duty that way, and you're also ready for any weather. Layering is especially useful in climates where the days are warm and the nights cool.

- Take one set of jewelry that will complement all outfits.

- Mix and match your outfits rather than planning a separate outfit for each day.

- Share hair dryers, curlers, and shampoo.

- ❏ comfortable walking shoes
- ❏ extra folding chair or two if you have a large group (You can use these indoors or out.)
- ❏ comfortable clothes (Layers are better; leave behind bulky items. See ideas in the "Lighten Your Luggage" sidebar.)
- ❏ makeup (Even though there is no one you need to impress, you may be horrified at your pictures and videos if you go au naturel for the weekend.)

 getaway gear

A MORE VERSATILE OUTFIT

As you're planning your getaway wardrobe, think about bringing a sarong (or pareu). It goes way beyond double duty to triple and quadruple duty. Here are 101 ways to wear one:

- long around your waist, as a beach cover or a skirt
- folded in half around your waist, as a short skirt
- wrapped twice around you and tied under your arms, as a strapless dress
- looped behind your neck, brought to the front and crossed over your chest to your back, then tied for a halter top
- as a scarf, à la Jackie O
- as a wrap, *pashmina*-style

Oh, that's not 101? What's sarong about that? (Yeah, we hear you groaning.)

- ❏ one simple, dressy outfit (For a special dinner out or if you plan a fun Hoity-Toity Night. See appendix 2.)
- ❏ a basic first-aid kit (bandages, bug-bite remedy, bug repellent, aloe vera gel for sunburn)
- ❏ extra toilet tissue, depending on how many are in your group (At least you can't accuse us of being unrealistic!)
- ❏ essential-oil room spray (See appendix 3.)
- ❏ gifts for your girlfriends
- ❏ add your own items:

....

....

....

....

....

....

....

....

In addition to a checklist, one of our sisters sends out two or three newsletters as our getaway weekend draws near. In them, she expresses her excitement at getting together again and then covers the details of the upcoming weekend: where we're going, what kinds of attractions are nearby, which of us is preparing which meals, what items to pack and what to leave behind.

These letters are great tools because they not only get us excited about the upcoming weekend, but they are also invaluable when it comes time to pack, since we're reminded of the location, weather patterns, and activities we have planned.

Planning a Great Time

Okay, you're packed. You've made your list and checked it twice. Have you thought about what you're going to do once you get to your "camp"? We realize that earlier we told you not to plan too much for your weekend, just to take it easy. Well, forget all that. No, really—we do want you to relax, take it easy, and enjoy simply being with your girlfriends. But we realize that you may be spending a day or more with women you've only talked to on the phone for the past few years. Can you imagine finally being in one another's company only to be confronted with awkward silence? Scary. So you might want to discuss ahead of time some activities that each of your girlfriends would like to do. Even if you see one another on a regular basis, you'll still need some planned diversions, and you'll want to do some things that you wouldn't normally do.

Breaking out of your routine makes your time together special. Use the ideas that follow as the stimulus to help you plan creative adventures and get your first getaway off to a great start. Remember, these are only suggestions. You should try just one or two of them. Don't bog yourself down with activities or you'll be in danger of spending the entire getaway checking items off your activities list.

A Welcoming Arrival

As Julie Andrews says in the *Sound of Music,* "Let's start at the very beginning, a very good place to start." For the best start possible, set the tone for your getaway by ensuring a pleasant arrival. A few simple, personal touches go a long way toward making every friend feel welcome and at home. But do this within reason. Don't go as far as the friends in the Decorating Club did. They arrived at their hotel suite and decided the room and its furnishings simply didn't measure up. They told us, "We were visually offended by the layout of the suite and were compelled to completely rearrange the sitting area. We considered leaving a calling card to say that 'The Decorating Club was here. No charge for the consultation!'" These women share a genuine appreciation for the delicate curve of a Chippendale chair, hence the name of their girlfriends' group. But unless you share that same appreciation, we don't expect you to take it that far. It's really about personalizing your getaway space and making it your own. If that means simply spraying your favorite (inoffensive) scent on the sheets, or changing them entirely, it's up to you.

Now that we're back to earth, let's talk about simple (and easy) touches that ensure a pleasant arrival. (For your first getaway, the responsibility will probably fall to you. But in years to come, every girlfriend will get her turn.) A warm welcome can involve something as simple as getting the room keys for everyone before they arrive, making sure the curtains are open and the room is aired out, and being there with your smiling face and open arms.

If you want to put forth a little more effort, you can put up a welcome sign, place fresh flowers on the desk or table, light a few scented candles, and have some favorite music playing. We like to hang a banner on the door of our condo that says, "Welcome to Sisters Weekend." You may want to make it more personal or even humorous: "Abandon All Business, Ye Who Enter Here," "Check Your Cell Phone at the Door," or "Girlfriends and Room Service Only Beyond This Point." The getaway is all about celebrating your sisterhood, so be creative. Since this adventure is yours and yours alone, reflect the personality of your group in the preparations for a warm and joyful welcome.

If you're feeling really ambitious, arrive early and put out a few simple snacks for everyone to munch on as they get settled. If you're like us and you've been in the car for a few hours, you'll probably be hungry by the time you arrive, and snacks get everyone comfortable and chatting. We don't like to structure the arrival time too much because this is our catch-up and letdown time. We all want to blurt out everything that's happening in our lives, tell funny stories about the trip, and talk about plans for the weekend. It's usually a cacophony of chatter and laughter, so don't frustrate yourself by trying to bring order where chaos is the rule.

The arrival time is important because it's when you and your friends slowly let go of everything you left behind—families, work, the demands of your daily lives—and start to sink into a time set aside for just being a girlfriend. It's kind of like sinking into an overstuffed chair. Just keep in mind that letting go may take more than one evening, especially on your first getaway. We often find that the "overstuffed chair" is just starting to feel really comfortable on the day that it's time to head back home. That's okay. In fact, it's one of the reasons you'll look forward to the following year's adventure. The main thing is to keep the first day or evening simple and unstructured.

Let your time unfold on its own, let the conversation go where it wants to, and just enjoy the fact that you are all together. If you encounter any awkward moments, just go with the flow and realize that this is a new thing for all of you, and it may have been a long time since you were all in the same room. Put on some fun music. The sound of favorite songs can make awkward silences not so silent and therefore not so awkward. Or play a board game such as Cranium, which sparks conversation, makes you laugh, and helps the barriers and defenses melt away as you act silly and don't really care. Chances are, once you're all together the problem won't be how to get the conversation going but when to stop talking and go to bed! Here's the bottom line: If you make your girlfriends feel welcome and at ease, your getaway is off to a great start.

Meal Planning

The all-important issue of what to eat is one that we tackle early in our getaway planning. Our meals together are some of the best times we share the entire weekend. More than once, we've found ourselves clutching at our stomachs, not because the food is bad, but because we're laughing so hard. So, to ensure a private, leisurely meal that everyone will enjoy, we cook our own.

We keep our food costs low and the workload reasonable by dividing into teams of two and making each team responsible for one day's meals. This actually turns out to be an easy task because we only have brunch and dinner. We begin with a simple "grazing" brunch that suits our style, since we greet the day slowly and sort of ease into the morning. (We often stay up until 2 A.M. the night before!) The big meal is dinner and can be whatever the team in charge wants it to be. If they don't want to cook, they can order out.

Arranging pairs of women to be in charge of each meal is easy, and everyone ends up enjoying culinary treats that rival the finest restaurants. (We admit there may be a bit of a competitive spirit here, so we pull out all the stops.) This plan also avoids the "too many cooks in the kitchen" crisis that could easily occur if we were all fending for ourselves. We have one final meal rule: The cooks never do cleanup. When their culinary masterpiece is complete, we shoo them out of the kitchen and the others take over.

A Wealth of Activities

There is no end to the range of activities you can consider for your time together. When we gather with our sisters, we usually spend a relaxing first evening and then plan one or two big events for the rest of the weekend. Sometimes we rent a boat for a day, since we're usually on or near a lake. If we're in a city, we attend a play. If your group has decided to eat most meals out, you can make selecting a restaurant part of your group's activities. Most women enjoy trying cuisine they wouldn't ordinarily eat at home, so consider a Moroccan or Indian restaurant, a sushi bar, or a fondue restaurant. And of course, if you're in a place, like Chicago, that's famous for a trademark dish, your meal choice is simple: deep-dish pizza!

It's easy to schedule one activity after another, but remember to leave some time open to be just plain crazy. Being crazy, we've found, is the only way to really let go of the insanity you deal with in your daily life. Writer and actress Nicole Johnson illustrates this perfectly: "Real laughter and enjoyment come from going deep and then rising to the surface to get air. The laughter is like bubbles on the way up."[1] Remember the Decorating Club we mentioned earlier? The group consists of only four people: two pairs of sisters. They not only enjoy decorating, they really enjoy being silly. For instance, they have taken the "club" concept to wonderful extremes by making up name tags, creating committee positions, and even printing up a membership directory. Along the way, they developed a prize for style and leadership called the "Golden Tassel Award," which they present to one another throughout the year. (We wonder if they shared this award for redecorating their hotel suite!)

"Our club has developed a bonding environment where we can tap into our creative, silly sides after being 'oh so grown up' in most other areas of our lives," these sisters tell us. "It's a very safe place for us to be totally ourselves in the silliest, most girlie kind of way. And it makes us laugh like nothing else!"

So as you plan the activities of your adventure, allow plenty of time to go nuts.

A SAMPLE ADVENTURE PLAN

As we write this book we are preparing for our annual Sisters Weekend. To help you come up with ideas for your own getaway, we've included a sample schedule of events. Participation in activities is always optional, and no doubt some of these will be dropped in favor of better ideas or unexpected opportunities that come along later. But it's a starting point that provides a little structure in planning as well as the benefit of dreaming about all the fun to come.

Day 1

10:00 A.M.—Arrive at destination

Gather at resort restaurant for "Here We Are!" brunch

Use pictures from last year's Sisters Weekends for table decoration

Sketch out weekend plans and the value for each girlfriend

Give sarongs to each girlfriend—the latest addition to our
Getaway Gear. (Our weekend paraphernalia started with sunglasses and hats for everyone. This was followed by T-shirts, pins, oxford shirts, necklaces, mugs, and glassware. Of course, to hold all this junk—we mean, treasure—we had to have bags. This year we'll add walking sticks and journals to the list, along with those sarongs.)

12:30 P.M.—Check in

    Pick bedrooms and unpack

    Relax on the deck with light snacks and conversation

    Hand out survival kits (See "The Survival Kit" sidebar.)

 k . i . s . s .

THE SURVIVAL KIT

To enhance your enjoyment and to help all of you stay organized, pack a survival kit. It consists of safety pins with name tags to clip on towels (saves on laundry and confusion) and ID tags for drinking glasses—they're just brightly colored rubber bands, a different color for each person. Embellish these any way you like. Now each person has one glass that's hers for the day!

The survival kit also includes a Memory Keeper, which is nothing more than a simple container—a film canister or a baby food jar. Place items in your Memory Keeper that symbolize a piece of your adventure that you want to keep the rest of the year. It could be a stone, a shell, a flower petal, a quotation, a verse of Scripture that speaks to your heart, or a memory or sensory experience that is symbolically "contained" in your Memory Keeper.

The last important part of the survival kit is a journal. Make your own for the weekend by using natural or colorful writing paper and corrugated cardboard for the cover. Punch three holes near the edge and tie with raffia. Record your thoughts and observations throughout your adventure. Make sure you write yourself an encouraging note to do this again soon!

6:00 P.M.—Evening Activities

    Dinner

    Entertainment

        "Cranium" board game

        Bonfires on the beach

        Hot tub

        Talk, talk, talk!

Day 2

"Morning Glories." Greet the morning with a little wisdom from the Scriptures and have each girlfriend write down her favorite Bible verses that are applicable to your time together. Roll them up, tie them with a pretty ribbon, and place them in a basket. First thing in the morning, everyone picks a scroll (or Morning Glory) to start their day. You can share your Glories with one another or keep them to yourselves to spark your journaling time.

9:00 A.M.—Exercise

10:00 A.M.—Brunch

12:00 P.M.—Outing (if the weather's nice)

6:00 P.M.—Evening activities

    Dinner

    Evening Entertainment (choose one or substitute your own):

        Infomercial Contest: If your group likes to ham it up, put on skits, and play games, try this one. We all know how annoying some infomercials are, so turn the tables and make up your own "products" to hawk to your group. They'll love the Exerciser that will tone you while you eat, the Instant Lip Plumper that you pump up "as needed" for your most glamorous you, or the toilet paper with a novel written on it called Read While You Roll. Make up your own; the funnier the better. There are only two rules: You have to use what's on hand, and you can't prepare ahead of time.

In-House Shopping Trip: A spin-off of the white elephant gift exchange, this is an auction with your treasured castoffs on the block. Everyone brings one fairly nice thing they don't want or need anymore. The others bid on it. The winner takes her prize and is out of the bidding. That way everyone gets to take home something fun and "new."

Watch the Northern Lights

Bonfires on the beach

More relaxing, talking, hot tubbing

Day 3
"Morning Glories"

9:00 A.M.—Exercise

10:00 A.M.—Brunch

12:00 P.M.—Go deeper (See description in chapter 6.)

Spa time (See appendix 3.)

Reflections and Prayer: Give every girlfriend a journal. The "reflections and prayer" segment is a time set aside to write in the journals, reflect on the weekend, pray, and for everyone to just be alone for a little while.

6:00 P.M.—Evening activities

Dinner

Entertainment
> Skits or games
>
> Sisterhood Singalong (See "The Sisterhood Singalong" side-bar for ideas.)
>
> Singing around the bonfire and listening to the night sounds of Lake Superior

Day 4 (departure morning)
"Morning Glories"
9:00 A.M.—Breakfast
10:00 A.M.—Winding down
> Make plans for next year
>
> Blessings over all: While others stand in a circle, each girlfriend takes a turn sitting in the middle. Pray over the one in the

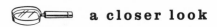 **a closer look**

THE SISTERHOOD SINGALONG

Singing together not only takes us back to our childhood family times, but it also creates a bond in the present. Whether it's a simple melody or complex harmony, singing unites us and sends us soaring. If one of your girlfriends plays an instrument you can sing along with, ask her to bring it, or just use a CD that will inspire you. Possibilities include camp songs, Top 40 hits from when you were teenagers, and praise choruses that have a special meaning for you.

---

middle—whatever comes to you, whatever that girlfriend needs in her life. Yes, tears flow, so if you're going to do this, have a box of tissues handy!

Pack up and head out!

A NOT-SO-SOLEMN INITIATION

Now that you have a general idea of what to do with your girlfriends once you get them together, there's just one more thing you have to do if you truly want to be part of the adventure. You guessed it—the initiation. We just happen to have one prepared for you.

The Girlfriends' Pledge

Raise your right big toe, pat your head, rub your stomach, and repeat after us: "I promise to uphold the values of the Girlfriends' Getaway adventure by seeing the beauty in my sisters and friends, encouraging them in their gifts, lifting them up in their time of need, engaging in silliness and hilarity, and participating in sistering moments as often and for as long as I am able."

Welcome to the adventure! (You may now lower your big toe and stop rubbing and patting.) Since you're now an official inductee of the circle of sisterhood, you can perform this initiation ceremony on fellow suckers, er, sisters. Just remember all of this is in good fun!

FIELD NOTES

Chapter 5

STOP FOR Lemonade

L E T L A U G H T E R Q U E N C H Y O U R S O U L

Laughter is the shortest distance between two people. —V I C T O R B O R G E

We really wanted to play a little joke on you in this chapter so you could experience firsthand the high jinks and hilarity that make up the soul of a Girlfriends' Getaway. Nothing too sneaky, mind you. We just wanted to print this page of type upside down so you'd look slightly ridiculous and confused as you tried to read it. But since we didn't want you to return your "damaged" book to the bookstore, we controlled ourselves.

The point is that it's the laughter at and with one another that refreshes our bonds, and we want you to get in on it! So take up the trickster torch and let it shine brightly. Leave your self-consciousness at home and enjoy some laughter, even at your own expense!

We have one sister who is particularly good at playing jokes (some may say *too* good). She'll burst into a room and scream, "Oh no! When did you get that huge dent in the side of your car?" and for a split second, you fall for it. Before you lose the horror-stricken look on your face, she yells, "Just kiddin'!"

 remedies

AIDING AND ABETTING CRAZINESS

Here are a few of our favorite, and exceedingly juvenile, props to rev up the laughs:

- *Fake doggie poo* (you knew we'd mention that, didn't you?). There are many ways to make the most of this. We used it to very good advantage on our first Sisters Weekend, and we have the photo to prove it: It shows a "delicate" little pile placed discretely next to a sleeping sister's head to help her dream of her lonesome pooch left behind for the very first time.

- *Whoopee cushion* (of course). We have a "love-hate" relationship with this thing and the sounds it makes. Again, we have proof—remember, we keep a video camera handy.

- *Fake (but all too real) spiders, snakes, and various other icky things.* Fun to use early in the morning or late at night when everyone's a little blurry eyed and not expecting to see creatures. Put them in sneaky places—dark corners, cupboards, drawers, suitcases, bathing suits, shoes. But don't get carried away; too many fakes lose their impact.

One year we decided to get even, so we purchased a large rubber—but very realistic—bug from a joke store and strategically placed it on a tree branch close to this sister's favorite lounge chair. We waited inside as she got comfortable out on the deck. It was only a few moments before we heard the screams, saw the door fly open, and knew we'd gotten our revenge. There she stood, with eyes as big as saucers and pure fright on her face. "Did you guys see that huge b-b-b-u-g…?" She didn't

- *Fake fly in the fake ice cube.* Lovely to find in a tall, cool drink while you're on the deck, by the pool, or somewhere outside. You'll hear the screams soon after the first sip!
- *Old home movies* (from when you were kids). Get ready for more laughs. The things you used to do when you were kids seem to get funnier and funnier the older you get. Watch for the hairdos, clothing, wallpaper, furniture, window treatments, and cars—yes, everything old eventually is new again (or at least twice as funny)!
- *Slumber party tricks.* Think back to junior high school and recall all your favorites: freezing underwear, black soap (that's really dirty!), shaving cream on the nose of a sleeping beauty, and the old standby, the sleeping-person's-hand-in-a-pan-of-warm-water trick.

And don't forget your own funny bone. Only you know what tickles you and your girlfriends. But remember to be sensitive, too. Even a funny bone hurts if hit the wrong way. The point is to laugh, not to make anyone feel bad!

even finish before we all burst into laughter. After a moment of disbelief, she laughed right along with us. It's a memory that still brings a smile to our faces.

Another year, to celebrate one sister's milestone birthday (we won't say *which* milestone or *which* sister), we took a pictorial romp through the history of her hairdos. Blown up to poster size were images of every era of her life, from childhood innocence to teen rebellion to mature glamour gal, as well as every color that hair can be dyed and every shape that it can be molded into. She's done it all, with style and grace to boot. There was a lot of laughter at her expense, but she laughed just as loudly as any of us and enjoyed every minute of her stroll down Hairspray Lane. What a girl!

But our own foolishness pales in comparison to other Girlfriends' Getaway shenanigans. We know one group of girlfriends who change their names on their getaways. This year they're using the names of flowers (Iris, Begonia, Salvia), and they're going to speak with an accent wherever they go (nationality yet to be determined). We assume it'll be something that sounds good with flower names.

When we were kids we used to pretend we were speaking another language. Do you remember doing this sort of thing long ago? You had no problem being a goofball back then (just ask your mother), so why not now? "Because it will make me look silly!" you say. Well, that's the whole point, girl. It's a widely accepted fact that children have a lot more fun than adults, so why not reclaim those days and be reminded of how much fun they were? Besides, as a wise and insightful guest on *Oprah* once said, "You wouldn't worry so much about what other people think of you if you knew how seldom they did."

So let's set aside our dignified adult habits for a moment and think about ways we can enjoy some uninhibited fun with our girlfriends.

The Pity Party

You're going to love this one. A friend told us about a stress-relieving activity she practices with a few close friends. It's called a Pity Party. As the name suggests, it starts off a little pathetically. Each participant arrives, as we all do, bearing the cares and burdens of daily life. There's all the unfairness, the unrealistic demands, the rushing around, and the continual annoyances to contend with. If it's not one thing, it's three other things.

During the first part of the evening, each friend spends some time wallowing in her own woes and telling everyone else all about it. Sometimes as the sad stories are told, it gets a little competitive. "You think *your* situation is bad, just wait until you hear about *mine!*"

Each woman shares her most pitiful story from the past year while she munches on Twinkies, red licorice, ice cream, Snickers bars, and all the other junk women deprive themselves of in their responsible lives. When everyone is finished gushing, the group votes for the girlfriend with the most pitiful story. The winner gets a basket filled with bath goodies, so she'll be better prepared to cope with her next really pitiful moment.

It doesn't end there. The friend who hosts the getaway takes the entire group to an even more pitiful level. She cues up scenes from certain videos ahead of time and then plays them for all to enjoy. She goes for the really sappy, overdone tragedies—the scenes that are so bad they're hilarious. After hearing one another's stories of self-pity and then watching bad actors portray even more tragic scenes, the whole group can't stop laughing. Each girlfriend soon realizes that her own problems aren't so serious after all. The Pity Party is healing and cathartic, something we all need once in a while. And on top of that, it's a lot of fun.

EMBARRASSING MOMENTS

Here's another idea that will guarantee a healthy laugh at yourself, but be ready to let go—it requires a bit of self-disclosure. Have friends sit in a circle and share their most embarrassing moments. True stories only, please. We bet you'll not only get a good laugh, but you'll learn something special about one another, too.

Since we're asking you to reveal an awkward moment, it's only fair that we go first. Here's a true, and somewhat embarrassing, story. Kathleen was once invited to a very elegant dance at an exclusive men's college. She dreamed about floating across the dance floor all evening with her Prince Charming and being treated like the royal princess she thought she was. After weeks of hunting all over, she found the perfect ball gown and then coordinated every detail of her ensemble, from earrings to shoes.

On the afternoon of the ball, she treated herself to a new "updo" at one of the city's finest beauty salons. This Princess for a Day enjoyed every minute of it, from the massaging shampoo to the relaxing hour spent under the hair drier. The warm, blowing air of the machine sent her into a contented stupor. She relaxed, closed her eyes, and sank back in the chair, letting go of time.

Suddenly she felt a hand lightly tap her arm as the hum of the hairdryer stopped and the sounds of the salon returned. "Time to make you beautiful!" the stylist said as she tipped the drier back and held out her hand to the slightly groggy girl, who took the proffered hand, stood up, and immediately fell to the floor! She had her legs crossed during her nap, cutting off the circulation to one leg. That leg had gone completely numb, and she couldn't stand on it. Not only that, but as feeling began to return, pain came with it. Her ankle soon began to swell, and her dreams of dancing in the arms of Prince Charming vanished. She'd be lucky if she could *limp* with Mr. Charming.

Yes, Kathleen the Princess still went to the ball that night, but she hobbled in on her date's arm and never once felt the joy of the dance. Pictures don't reveal the whole truth of this glamorous event. They show the lovely curls piled high on her head, the elegant earrings shimmering in the light, and the glowing smile on her face. But the complete truth is hidden under her beautiful, flowing dress in the form of a big, fat, purple foot that never ever fit into a glass slipper.

Now it's your turn. Think about *your* most embarrassing moment and get ready to share. If we can publicly spill our most embarrassing moments, you can do it too, and you only have to tell your best girlfriends.

The Rewards of Laughter

We'd never be happy with a life that didn't include a little craziness. We're two grown women, so why do we emphasize this seemingly juvenile indulgence? Because it's only after you've laughed yourself silly that you can begin to open up and be genuine—no facades, no false pride, no masks that hide who you really are. On a Girlfriends' Getaway, no fake girlfriends are allowed. We're open and accepting of one another. And opening up sometimes means telling about blunders and foibles and other things we usually try to pretend didn't happen. Not only is getting it out there entertaining for others, it brings healing to the woman who's revealing something about herself. You'll be surprised at how liberated you feel after a fit of uncontrollable laughter.

In many cases, laughter truly is the best medicine. And laughing at oneself may be the best prescription of all. So go ahead, blush a little, feel ridiculous a little, live a little! This is a juvenile indulgence, so be a kid again. What have you got to lose but that well-composed, well-meaning, but boring adult image?

FIELD NOTES

Chapter 6

DIG FOR TREASURE

DISCOVER THE REWARDS OF GOING DEEPER

Therefore encourage one another and build each other up,
just as in fact you are doing. — I THESSALONIANS 5:11

Up to now, we've given you a vision of a getaway that is filled with laughter, joy, relaxation, and play. But the heart of the adventure begins the moment you start exploring deeper relationships with one another.

In her book *Wit and Wisdom for Women,* Barbara Jenkins advises,

All women are born with the need to communicate at a deeper level with their mothers, grandmothers, sisters, daughters, aunts, cousins, and other significant females in their lives. Friends remind us we are part of something greater than ourselves, a larger world, and the right friends keep us on track. Now is the time to reclaim and reestablish ourselves as friends.[1]

This is the heart and soul of a Girlfriends' Getaway. This is what's really going on behind all the activity. And this is the life-changing adventure we desire for you.

The women in our group are related, so we've known one another all our lives. As girls, we fought over the bathroom and struggled through the typical childhood stages. Yet when we get together, we still need a time of connecting through lighthearted fun before we're ready to slow down and share on a deeper level. The laughter and silliness we indulge in help us shed the roles we fill in everyday life. We naturally bring those roles to our weekends, but we also know we can't reveal the deeper parts of ourselves until we drop the facade and get honest.

HOW TO GO DEEPER

As the organizer of your Girlfriends' Getaway, you have the clearest idea of what you hope to accomplish during your time together. You want the group to do more than just have fun. You want each person to let down her defenses, share openly, and reach out to the others with sisterly support. All of that is essential, so don't lose sight of the goal. But realize also that you'll need to be patient. A successful getaway depends on a flexible agenda. Some of your girlfriends may not be ready to share what's really on their hearts. You can't force self-disclosure, but you can invite it and gently encourage it. Be patient, loving, and sensitive to the moods of your girlfriends.

There are ways to encourage openness. To help each one feel the freedom to reveal a deeper part of herself, try this simple exercise. It starts off almost like a game but can develop into meaningful sharing. When you're relaxing on the beach or in front of the fireplace, share answers to these thought-provoking questions:

- When you were a very young child, what did you want to be when you grew up?
- When you were growing up, what did you get into trouble for more often than anything else?
- Suppose a movie were to be made about your life. Who do you think would be best suited to play you in the film, and why?
- What is the silliest, most off-the-wall thing you've ever done?
- What is the most valuable fact or insight you've learned in the last year?
- How is God using your unique design these days?

For more great questions, check out *The Book of Questions,* by Gregory Stock, Ph.D.[2] It's full of questions that promote deeper conversation and help you get to know the sometimes-hidden sides of your girlfriends.

If the Shoe Fits

If asking and answering questions out of a book seems too formulaic, you can prompt deeper conversation by using another device: a shoe. Actually, one shoe from each friend in your group.

Before you gather, ask each woman to bring along a shoe. Not an ordinary shoe, but one that has a story behind it. Your girlfriends will probably show up with saddle oxfords, toe shoes or tap shoes, high-top basketball shoes, Mary Janes, golf shoes, hiking boots, western boots, or even glittery spike heels. The shoe itself isn't important; it's the story behind the shoe that counts. Have each woman present her shoe and then explain why she brought it. Maybe it's a white slipper she wore on her wedding day or a hiking boot she was wearing when she got hopelessly lost in the Alaskan wilderness. Maybe it's the spike heel she was wearing the night her old boyfriend broke her heart.

Each shoe represents a significant life event, a trauma or a blessing. It could be a tragedy that has now turned into a source of strength. It could be a rite of passage that set a course for the storyteller's adult life. The shoe could symbolize an experience that led the girlfriend to a new insight into herself or others. It doesn't matter if the story is humorous or heart wrenching. The richness comes from telling one another something important about your lives. The shoe circle is a way to help your friends think about their lives in a new way and share those insights with a group of women who care about them. It's a nonthreatening way to invite deeper sharing.

THE SIGNIFICANCE OF LISTENING

No matter what method you use to help get everyone talking, it's important that each member of your group has the chance to be heard. And that takes time. If you have more than four girlfriends, you'll need to be extra sensitive to this. Talkative friends can get so caught up in telling a story that they use up the available time. And friends who are shy will never demand the floor. They're much more likely to remain quiet, thinking their own stories are less interesting or less important than the others.

You may find yourself being the facilitator. Make sure you allow each person to share something that is meaningful to her. If she doesn't want to talk about something that is deeply personal, she can simply share a piece of music she recently discovered or an inspiring book she read in the last year. Someone else may want to share an experience that blessed or challenged her. The most important thing is that *everyone* must have the chance to shine. Give the last speaker the same attention as the first. By eagerly listening, giving your attention, and asking appropriate questions, you are affirming one another and showing you care.

We all know that good communication is made up of two parts: talking and listening. But it's easy to concentrate so much on the talking half that we neglect the importance of careful, active listening. Developing the skill of listening leads to understanding and is key to mastering the art of communication.

Listening involves commitment. It says, "You are more important than I am at this moment. I care about you and what's going on in your life." When you're in a group situation, it takes forethought and agreement to stay focused on one person at a time and allow that friend the freedom she needs to express herself. Take the thirteen friends from high school and college that we mentioned in chapter 1. Because of the size of their group, one of the women sent out notes several days before their weekend, reminding the women of their previous agreement: They would set aside time to hear what had been happening in each person's life. So they all came prepared to share and listen.

They sat in a circle, eager to hear what had taken place since they had last been together. Can you imagine the scene? Thirteen women sitting cross-legged on the cabin floor, the furniture pushed back to make room for them all, the light from the fireplace flickering on their faces as they lean forward, not wanting to miss a word. They've told us that this process takes several hours, and by the time the last girlfriend speaks, it's early morning. They've got listening stamina!

Another important listening skill is maintaining eye contact. You know how annoying and hurtful it is to be pouring out your heart and realize you're having a conversation only with yourself because no one is looking at you. The old saying that the eye is the window to the soul depicts how looking into someone's eyes can lead to learning more about that person.

Sometimes when I (Kathleen) was young, my mom would try to tell me something important, but I was too busy to listen. So she'd grab me by the shoulders, bend down to look me in the face, and say something like "Please look at me when I speak to you." She wanted to make sure I understood her. It's the same for our friends. If we want to build confidence and trust, we need to grant each person value and respect by looking at her with interest when she speaks. When you look someone in the eyes, you will often see what she is *really* trying to tell you behind the words she is using.

In addition to maintaining eye contact when we are listening, we need to be aware of our tendency to interrupt the speaker with our own comments. Have you ever talked to someone who kept interrupting you, often in order to direct the conversation back to herself? You're probably rolling your eyes at the very thought! It's important to stay quiet when another person is talking, unless, of course, you're rephrasing what you hear to make sure you understood correctly. This, too, gives value to the person speaking.

During one of our first times of going deeper with our sisters, we found it difficult to stay on track. It seemed to take us forever to go around the circle. For example, one sister would begin to respond to the question, "When you were a very young child, what did you want to be when you grew up?" And before she had even gotten her answer out, someone would make a witty comment, laughter would break out, and we were off on another tangent. It took a concentrated effort to stay the course and focus on the individual, giving each one the time she needed to be vulnerable and divulge her heart's desires. But by doing so, we learned some important lessons. One sweet sister revealed that her childhood dream to be a singer had been squelched early on by an insensitive (and clueless) teacher who, after an audition for the school play, told our sister she would never be good enough. Another sister shared her goal to be the first woman on the moon. We say both dreams are still possible!

Finally, when it comes to listening, sometimes sharing a few moments of silence can be the most powerful way of going deeper. A friend from Colorado describes her experience beautifully.

This time is very important to me because it is six women sitting quietly in a room of comfortable chairs and sofas with afghans and dimmed lights, closing our eyes and being quiet within ourselves, yet knowing we are fully supported by all of the other women in the room. It is a very peaceful and safe environment, and I feel fortunate to be a part of such a wonderful experience.

All we can say is, "Ahhh."

HEARTFELT PRAISE

So far we've considered how to get your girlfriends to share the deeper parts of themselves. But there is a second way to open up to one another that has nothing to do with revealing your own secrets. It involves expressing what we truly admire about one another.

One year, a few months before we gathered for our annual Sisters Weekend, each of us received eight blank note cards. We were asked to list all the positive qualities we saw in each sister, using one card per sister. Then on a quiet evening of our weekend, as we sprawled in a large, comfortable bedroom, we took turns reading aloud to each sister the many good qualities we recognized and admired in her. It was a rare life-changing experience and a moment we mark as a turning point in the power and value of our times together.

Because this exercise was so valuable for us, we decided to extend the blessing to our spouses. What marriage isn't strengthened by hearing others confirm the strengths and other positive qualities of your mate? By reading aloud to each sister what good things we saw in *her* husband, we were encouraged and united even more. And each of us came away from it with a new appreciation for our better half. We went home from that weekend and told our husbands how much we, and our sisters, valued them. I (Kathleen) was reminded, among other things, that my husband is patient and faithful, and that he has a great smile. Of course, I knew these things already. But it had been a while since I'd communicated to him how much it meant to me that he is so dependable in every circumstance, that he has been true to me for more than thirty years, and that he is handsome, too!

When we got home and read these blessings to our men, we were able to pass one of our Sisters Weekend treasures on to someone outside the circle. You could do the same thing with your children or a close friend or anyone else who is important to you.

A Place of Safety and Support

The real power of being together is the rich opportunity to learn more about one another as we share our hearts in a community of support and safety. This is the time we take the risk of being open with one another and wrap ourselves around one another's hearts and souls. It's a time to speak and listen, to share and nurture. This is when mentoring takes place, as we exchange wisdom and request input. We affirm the value of each individual, and we encourage each sister's desire to grow, to take risks, to try things that might be a little uncomfortable at first.

The deeper sharing that takes place helps us refresh our spirits and renew bonds of faith that connect us in ways more important than friendship, even more important than flesh and blood. It's during this time that we share our gifts of grace, our stumbles and failures, our successes and joys. It's also when we share manifestations of God's love for us and our families. It's the time we support one another in our struggles and in our endeavors to be strong and faithful women—faithful in our relationships and faithful in following God.

The result of all this sharing is health and new strength, both for the individual and for her family and community. Since women tend to be the keepers of relationships, traditions, and values, both in families and in communities, strong women ultimately contribute to a strong and healthy society. The benefits of women spending meaningful time with one another radiate out to others far beyond the circle of sisters.

One sister puts it this way:

A by-product of getting away together is understanding the need for other people, outside the family, in our lives. As we grow to understand and accept the need to allow others into the deeper parts of our lives, we allow the intimacy to increase and become more important and necessary to our complete well-being. It is not dependence so much as survival of the heart.

This woman has put her discovery into action. She started a book discussion group in her neighborhood, establishing a common bond among former strangers. She also responded to the urgent call of her church when a local couple that had just had quintuplets needed help with the care of their newborns. The bonds that have formed between this woman and the family she helped are deep and lasting. She has been a blessing to them and they to her.

Even taking the risk of writing this book has come out of our Sisters Weekend experiences. The idea, the desire to encourage women to experience what we have experienced, and the courage to commit and follow through were all born out of the strength and inspiration we have derived from the strong company of our sisters.

"Our challenge then is to say yes to the most important things, the things for which God has brought us to this time and place," says author and Bible teacher Ruth Haley Barton. "In so doing we make room in our lives for meaning and value, and we will feel God's pleasure upon us.... Will it be risky? More so than staying in a quiet harbor. Will it be exhilarating? You bet! Will it be fulfilling? Well, let's put it this way: It's the only way to live."[3]

We invite you to take on this challenge with your girlfriends. You may not be ready for it on your very first getaway. But at some point—you'll know when—you and your girlfriends will need to take this step of faith with one another, and when you do you'll find that it really is the only way to live.

Deeper Bonds Through Prayer

As your getaway winds down and you start preparing to return home, make sure you end your time together with something that will last. Spend the final moments before departing for home in prayer for one another. Make it personal by going through the group one by one and having the others pray specifically for that friend. To make it even more meaningful, have one friend at a time sit in the middle of a circle while the others stand around her, asking blessings over her until you gather again.

The first year we did this with our sisters, we received an alarming phone call just as we were finishing our blessings. A relative had been in a terrible accident and narrowly escaped being killed. He was on a construction site when a large dump truck filled with sand tipped over and struck him, breaking his back. Because we were all together, we were able to pray for him as we were praying for one another. It was a powerful moment for us as a family. Our relative has made a slow but miraculous recovery, and we have never missed a time of prayer before departing for home since then!

If you're not used to praying spontaneously, or if the idea of praying aloud is a bit daunting, following are some written prayers you can use. If you want to, you can personalize them by inserting the name of the girlfriend you're praying for.

Irish Blessing

May the road rise to meet you,

May the wind be always at your back,

May the sun shine warm on your face,

The rain fall softly on your fields;

And until we meet again,

May God hold you in the palm of his hand.

Traditional Blessing

The LORD bless you

and keep you;

the LORD make his face shine upon you

and be gracious to you;

the LORD turn his face toward you

and give you peace. (Numbers 6:24-26)

Another way to prompt prayers is to pray together, telling God what you are most thankful for. You can thank him for the many blessings he has brought about in your life and for your girlfriends and what they bring to your life.

If you need additional inspiration for your times of prayer and reflection, try some of the suggestions in the "Personal Reflection" and "Prayers of Thanksgiving" sidebars on the following pages.

Whether you pray spontaneously as the Spirit leads or use a written prayer that believers have prayed through the ages, we encourage you to take this time of inspiration before your getaway ends. You'll find that it gives new meaning and depth to your adventure.

remedies

Personal Reflection

Provide an opportunity for quiet time during your Girlfriends' Getaway. It's best to do this in the morning, since once you're into a lively day, it's hard to shift gears. Bring small spiral notebooks or bound journals, set aside a time of solitude and then, if desired, come back together to share what you discovered. You may want to take a scripture verse or an inspirational quote with you for reflection (see following samples).

If I rise on the wings of the dawn,
>   if I settle on the far side of the sea,
even there your hand will guide me,
>   your right hand will hold me fast. (Psalm 139:9-10)

The LORD your God is with you,
>   he is mighty to save.
He will take great delight in you,
>   he will quiet you with his love,
>   he will rejoice over you with singing. (Zephaniah 3:17)

The real voyage of discovery consists not in seeking new
>   landscapes but in having new eyes. —Marcel Proust

The beginning is always today. —Mary Wollstonecraft

remedies

PRAYERS OF THANKSGIVING

There's an old French proverb that says, "Gratitude is the heart's memory." Thankfulness promotes positive attitudes and is a great way to start a time of inspiration. From the following list, choose a few things you're most thankful for and share them with one another during a time of prayer.

- calling
- character
- church
- courage
- creativity
- faith
- family
- friends
- future
- health
- heritage
- home
- job
- neighborhood
- school
- sense of purpose
- talents
- wisdom

FIELD NOTES

DIAMOND OR LUMP OF COAL?

WHAT TO DO IF YOUR GETAWAY DISAPPOINTS YOU

The way I see it, if you want the rainbow,
you gotta put up with the rain. —DOLLY PARTON

Y ou know that it takes a lot of digging to find diamonds. Getting at these precious stones requires determination, effort, and back-breaking work. Hidden deep in the earth, diamonds are one of the hardest stones known to man. And even when they are brought to the surface they need to be properly handled—meticulously cut and polished—to become the brilliant, beautiful gems we treasure.

Most of the time, life is bliss when you're on a Girlfriends' Getaway.

But sometimes, like diamonds, the enjoyment comes only after generous amounts of hard work, perseverance, and careful handling. We hope you'll never need to use the advice in this chapter. However, we all live in the real world, and we want you to know that if something does go wrong, you're not alone. Most of all, we want to give you the tools to work things out so you won't give up on your great adventure.

Remember Judy from chapter 2? She and her sisters found themselves getting into petty arguments that dated back to childhood. Same arguments, different subject matter. For example, instead of fighting over one sister getting a nicer Christmas present, they'd wrestle over life accomplishments, secretly hoping to one-up the other. Deep down, they knew this was happening, but they didn't want to get to the bottom of it. They just wanted to forget about it once their getaway weekend was over. Had they just taken a little time before or during their

 **a closer look**

THE VALUE OF CONFLICT

Conflict is stressful and trying, but not all conflict is bad. Consider the words of poet and author Maya Angelou: "Surviving is important, but thriving is *elegant*."[1] You can bet Ms. Angelou has had her share of conflicts, but they've made her who she is today. When you help yourself or your girlfriends address and work through conflict, you're helping them not just to survive, but to *thrive!*

getaway to candidly discuss what was happening, they might have had a more successful and satisfying time together. A few conflict-resolution skills go a long way toward turning a would-be disaster into a richer and deeper experience for everyone.

We know a group of women who are blessed with a wonderful relationship, precious and rock solid. So they were deeply shocked when they experienced real conflict on one of their getaways. Unmet expectations, faulty communication, and big life stresses all conspired to create a bomb that didn't take long to explode. For a few hours, they thought the weekend was over.

One of the friends, Mary, brought the sting of a marriage in trouble to the enchanting hotel on the ocean where they were staying. Despite the loving efforts of the others and the beauty of the surroundings, she wasn't able to fully engage in the fun of this particular adventure. But Mary wasn't the only one who was struggling. Susan was dealing with her own stress, a life-threatening health problem in her immediate family. She valiantly tried to put it behind her as the weekend began, but the worries, pressures, and frustrations of her life back home weighed heavily on her. And somehow, the weekend itself was stressful for both of them. Wasn't this supposed to be the stress *reliever,* the magic potion to make it all go away—at least for a little while? Well, the stress wasn't going away, and they both knew that back home they were going to face the same big issues.

The tension in the lovely beach hotel was evident to everyone, but they continued on with their weekend plans until the second day, when a minor communication glitch escalated into a full-blown argument. Nothing even close to this had ever taken place on their weekends before. Everyone was in shock until one of the friends initiated the process of talking it out.

It took determination, patience, and open hearts to address some of the issues, but these friends stayed the course and lovingly salvaged what time remained. They learned some valuable lessons about themselves and one another in the aftermath of their conflict. Each woman came away with a new perspective on the burdens each of the others carried. They were reminded of their own fallibility, and they learned that no one is perfect and things are bound to go wrong sometimes.

A Girlfriends' Getaway isn't the panacea for the struggles we face. It's a great shot in the arm, no question. But if we expect it to solve all our problems, we'll doom the experience to failure. Sometimes personal expectations or stresses from home can cause us to be less than the unconditionally loving sisters or friends we usually are. When that's the case, we might not extend or receive the grace that we typically do.

Take the Initiative

Some problems can be avoided by thinking through possible tension points ahead of time. If you anticipate potential causes of tension, do what you can before the getaway begins to address simmering conflicts and unrealistic expectations.

A friend of ours who's a getaway veteran sensed some uneasiness with one of the sisters in her group before their weekend began. A few weeks earlier she had asked this sister to consider sharing some personal insights and lessons from her life during their getaway. After issuing that invitation, our friend found out that her sister had lost interest in even attending the weekend. A few days before they were to leave, she gently approached the sister. They went out for coffee and talked through their concerns about this aspect of the weekend. The sister admitted that she was reluctant to open up and become so vulnerable about these aspects of her life. Our friend was able to reassure her and provide the support and encouragement she needed. With foresight, a little time, and the right attitude, they were able to resolve the feelings that could have been a barrier to a fulfilling and rich weekend for them all.

COMMON FRICTION POINTS

It helps to be aware of what often causes friction at a Girlfriends' Getaway. The most common factors that work against a successful getaway can be counted on one hand. Once we recognize them and understand what's behind them, we can take steps to minimize their impact. Let's look at them one by one.

Unrealistic Expectations

Loading the weekend down with impossible goals, thinking a getaway will solve all your problems, hoping you'll take care of all the unfinished business that has built up over a lifetime—all of these expectations can destroy a getaway adventure.

Sometimes, when our lives are particularly stressful, we tend to place undue importance on events such as a Girlfriends' Getaway. We look forward to escaping from a hectic pace and basking in relaxation, but we can build up these escapes in our minds so much that there's no way our expectations could realistically be met. Then we feel disappointed. But instead of admitting our disappointment, we may lash out in anger or frustration. A Girlfriends' Getaway is a wonderful time, but it's not a *perfect* time. Keeping that in mind, especially before your first getaway, may help you avoid this potential source of conflict.

Faulty Communication

Misunderstandings, oversensitivity, projecting personal feelings onto another person, reading into comments what's not really there—these types of miscommunication can all lead to conflict. The best way to

 bumps and bruises

TALK THINGS OUT

These suggestions will help you resolve simple conflicts. If members of your group have serious issues, encourage them to seek counseling. To address more routine types of conflict, try these strategies:

- Listen first, carefully, without thinking about how you'll respond. After the person is finished talking, then respond.

- Try to see things from the other person's point of view, even if you're convinced that you're right. (Isn't it the certainty that *we're* right that gets us into trouble in the first place?)

- Begin your comments with "I feel_____" rather than "You make me feel_____." Clear up miscommunication with, "I'm hearing you say_____ (fill in the blank). Is that what you mean?"

- Ask for and extend forgiveness, if necessary. Conflict doesn't always get resolved in a nice, neat package. Sometimes someone just has to be forgiven, even if the hurt is still there.

resolve miscommunication is to take intentional steps to clarify what was said. When you sense that someone has misunderstood your words or deeds, restate what you meant to say. Don't let misunderstandings go unresolved once you recognize them. And if you think that you may be misinterpreting someone else, ask her to clarify what she just said.

Sorting through bad communication is never easy, but it's always worthwhile. A great deal of hurt, blame, and hard feelings can be avoided simply by opening the channels of communication.

Assuming Girlfriends Are Mind Readers

Many people, ourselves included, are in the habit of keeping things bottled up inside and then expecting others to know how we're feeling and what we need—basically, expecting everyone around us to read our minds. Well, despite what the infomercial psychics want you to believe, no human can read minds, and expecting this supernatural ability from our sisters and girlfriends is unfair and can lead to frustration, disappointment, and anger. It may not be easy admitting to your friends that you feel grumpy, vulnerable, scared, or weak, but believe us, you'll feel better knowing that you've helped them understand you. As Martha Stewart would say, "It's a good thing."

Life Stresses

Bringing extreme anger, feelings of victimization, fear, or stress into the weekend is possibly the most common and quickest way to ruin your getaway. We all have stresses in our lives, but sometimes one or more of your girlfriends may be facing Uber-stress. This kind of stress goes beyond the normal, day-to-day stresses and is experienced when a friend catches her husband cheating, loses her job, finds out her closest sibling is terminally ill, or is grieving a death in the family. We've faced stresses such as these during our getaways, and, at one time or another, you will too. Dealing with these kinds of situations takes extreme sensitivity on the part of the group, and there is no cut-and-dried solution.

You may want to have some time with a girlfriend before the getaway to talk about a difficulty she's dealing with. Talking it out ahead of time will help her leave it behind during the getaway. Or you may wish to designate some time during the getaway for her to let it all out. That's a decision you'll have to make based on what your friend is comfortable with. On the other hand, she may not wish to talk about it, either before or during the getaway, and that's something the rest of you will have to respect. Understand that she may be on edge, so try to give her a little space. Let her know that when *she* is ready, you are there for her.

Old, Unresolved Issues

There may be childhood issues or simply issues between friends that have never been addressed and have just been left to fester underneath the surface. In situations like these, the Girlfriends' Getaway acts like a hot house, causing otherwise innocuous weeds to grow and possibly take over the garden. Head off disaster by confronting these issues before your weekend if possible. Otherwise, simply being aware of them may be enough. Awareness will help you catch yourself or others when you see friends falling into old habits or roles, and you can then make a correction before conflict even begins. (For additional pointers on recognizing and heading off potential problems before your getaway adventure starts, take The Conflict Catcher Quiz in the following sidebar to find out whether your group may be at risk for conflict.)

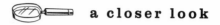 **a closer look**

The Conflict Catcher Quiz

Is conflict headed your way? Find out by taking this simple quiz:

- Has a major life event (good or bad) occurred in your life (or in the life of one of your girlfriends) in the last three months?
- Has there been a confrontation between two or more girlfriends in the past month?
- Has your group tried getting together in the past and have some friends been disappointed with the results?
- Do the girlfriends in your group have strong or very different personalities?
- Has it been a challenge for your friends to agree to go on a getaway together?
- Does one or more of your girlfriends lead a highly stressful life? (She may be a single mom or have a very stressful job.)

If you answered "yes" to one question, you might want to prepare your group for possible conflict. If you answered "yes" to two questions, you should try to address potential problems before your getaway begins. If you answered "yes" to three or more questions, you may want to delay your getaway until a calmer time, or you may want to choose different girlfriends for your getaway this time. Or you might decide to proceed with your plans anyway. Sometimes the positive results of a getaway outweigh the negative ones, and if you are committed to work through any conflicts, by all means, go for it.

The Truth About Solutions

Most of the big life challenges that we struggle with require time, wisdom, counsel, and the healing work of God before we find true resolution. Few problems can be solved in just one weekend. So helping one another recognize that there is no magical fix for everything is a step in the right direction. But providing support, being a careful and empathic listener, and gathering around a sister to offer prayer and comfort will go a long way to directing her to a lasting solution. You can offer real help during a Girlfriends' Getaway, but make sure no one is coming to the adventure looking for a complete cure.

Try to help clarify for each girlfriend ahead of time what the weekend can reasonably be expected to accomplish and what it can't possibly deliver. Lovingly address any areas of conflict that arise during the planning stage. Be sensitive to personality conflicts and other potential sources of tension.

Most women are usually so overjoyed to get away from the routines of life so they can enjoy time with their closest friends that they are more generous, more forgiving, and more accepting of circumstances that don't go entirely their way. The spirit of sisterhood and the joy of time together have a way of minimizing irritants that might push them over the edge if they occurred at home or at work. So, in most cases, the advice in this chapter is never needed.

Still, when things blow up in a big scene or disintegrate into a fit of weeping and withdrawal, it's distressing for even the most confident of girlfriends. It's hard, we know. But if your getaway adventure doesn't go quite the way you'd like it to, don't despair and don't give up. You and your girlfriends are human. The important thing is that you take the initiative to sensitively address any conflicts and then move on.

Knowing how to resolve conflict is a valuable skill that you'll be able to use often while walking life's bumpy trail. And remember, a lump of coal is nothing but a diamond waiting to happen.

FIELD NOTES

PART III | GET GOING

Chapter 8

enJOY THE RICHes

THE ONGOING GIFT OF GIRLFRIENDS

Look ahead because you can't get very far
looking in the rearview mirror. — BARBARA JENKINS

I t's not enough to have a Girlfriends' Getaway. It's like eating potato chips—you can't stop with just one. From the moment we ended our first weekend adventure, we couldn't wait for the next. That first experience was an awesome thing: the six of us together with no responsibilities, no children, no deadlines, no appointments—just us. We had tasted an amazing, life-altering adventure, and we wanted more.

On the morning of our last day together, plans for our next adventure began to form. Before we knew it we had picked a date, reserved a hotel suite, and discussed what we'd do differently the following year to make sure the fun would go on. (At the top of the list were a bigger room, a second bathroom, and more beds.)

As the years have gone by, we've found that we love everything about our annual weekend adventure. We revel in acting silly—the days overflow with laughter, practical jokes, and wild antics. We satisfy our hunger for personal sharing—the nights are filled with hours of reminiscing and philosophizing. We rarely mention our families, our problems, or our jobs, which surprises us. You know it's almost a requirement for mothers to get together and obsess over their kids. And it's easy for the stresses of life and the responsibilities of work to dominate thoughts and conversations. But we don't let that happen during this time we share together. Instead, we spend our time rediscovering one another.

We sing, dance, laugh, and cry. Mostly we laugh. We create wonderful meals to savor, and we soak in the warmth of the sun and giggle at the amusing, touching, honest stories we tell. We watch old movies and stage funny skits. We share beauty secrets and exchange simple gifts. We relive memories of childhood and share visions of the future. And then we laugh some more. (Yes, those good endorphins work overtime!) But we also slow down to absorb the treasure we have found in one another and in God. We share the deeper sides of ourselves and listen to one another's hopes and dreams.

BENEFITS ALL YEAR LONG

What have all of these good feelings really done for us? We could write several volumes on the subject, but we won't. Instead, we'll tell you a couple of quick stories.

One of the best things about a weekend with our sisters is discovering new things about one another. On our first getaway we had a delightful surprise as one of our sisters revealed remarkable powers of mimicry coupled with a brilliant sense of humor. She kept us entertained with her vast repertoire of crazy characters and foreign accents, and all the while we wondered if this was really our sister or a very clever imposter. But every year this "imposter" returns, and now she's

 remedies

THE BEAUTY OF CELLULOID

Celluloid (celluloid, not cellu*lite*) is a great way to bring on a bonding moment. For a memorable Chick Flick Night, put on your pj's, pop some corn, and get out the tissues! Here are a couple of our faves:

An Affair to Remember, starring Cary Grant and Deborah Kerr. Set in the elegant fifties, this classic brings together a beautiful singer and a handsome ladies' man. The respect displayed between the strong main characters is beautiful as they demonstrate the power of love and self-sacrifice. You'll never look at the Empire State Building in the same way again.

Enchanted April, starring Joan Plowright. Set in the 1920s, this film tells the story of a group of women whose only connection is their shared longing to trade the wet, dark London spring for the warmth and sun of the Mediterranean. This film is a great illustration of the power of sistering. It will spark some good postfilm conversation, as well as leave you with a sunny heart.

even making appearances outside of our annual weekend getaways. This woman is in her forties, and fifty-one weekends of the year she's a responsible mom, wife, and coworker. But turn her loose with her sisters, and she puts on a show you wouldn't believe. Give her any props—a curly blond wig, a military hat, or fake teeth—and anyone from Harpo Marx to General Patton to Jerry Lewis could show up. Even when she's not sending us into fits of laughter, she's a more lighthearted, happier version of herself when we get together. The rest of us enjoy the benefits of nonstop hilarity while appreciating and encouraging her delightful talent.

But our group isn't the only one that has uncovered new faces among the weekend sorority. Another group of women created Laugh In, a stress-relieving outlet involving sisters and cousins. They describe themselves as "good, hearty laughers" and have found a welcome security when they get together. Gathering for one weekend a year has helped them maintain strong ties in this mobile society. One of their favorite activities is telling stories about past generations of women in their family. But they don't stop at merely telling stories. They actually dress up in period costumes.

Recently one of these Scandinavian ancestors made a special appearance to delight more than just the Laugh In group. "Auntie," already well known to the Laugh In gals, attended a family wedding. Wobbling across the dance floor during the reception, she captured the attention of every guest, for this was not your typical auntie but a woman from another time and place. She wore a saggy print dress, loose baggy nylons, a hat with a veil, a stuffed bra, and high heels that she could barely control. This costumed Laugh In sister leaned on the piano and sang an old love song for the startled bridal couple, taking them and all their guests from laughter to tears. That face, form, and voice is something no one at the party will ever forget.

Through getting together for their weekends, these laughing ladies have not only benefited from their stress-relieving creativity, but they have also gained a special appreciation for where they came from and who they are. They've begun to see how they fit into a larger picture— a legacy of women that spans generations and culminates in each of them but will also go on for decades to come.

Bonding with one another during a Girlfriends' Getaway adventure takes many forms. One group settled on garishly decorated sunglasses as their identifying mark. Then they proudly wore them as they strutted through town together. The shades they wore had been lovingly crafted for each of them. The oldest (she dislikes that term, preferring firstborn) donned her pair of sunglasses—silk flower petals perched on the rims as if they were lashes coated with nature's mascara. Another sparkled as her set, coated with colorful sequins, glistened and danced in the sun, making her look like a young starlet. All six pairs of glasses were unique and flamboyant—a little like their new owners. These women attracted plenty of attention as they walked together, and they discovered to their surprise that they liked it.

As they sashayed through town, however, they weren't prepared for what was about to happen: They were stopped everywhere with questions about "those fabulous glasses!"

"Where did you get them? Where can I buy them?"

Unfortunately, there were only six pairs in existence, and they were created for these sisters alone. Many disappointed faces populated the town that day, but six proud heads were held high! (For ideas on creating memorable girlfriends' glasses, see the Getaway Gear sidebar, "Eye-Popping Sunglasses.")

THE STRENGTH OF BELONGING

There's a certain permanence and reassurance that comes from feeling a part of something greater than yourself. There's a comfort, as we've said before, but also a pool of strength that you can draw from after you return home. Remember the term sistering from the building trades—the joining of two boards to strengthen one where it was weak. As one

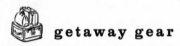 **getaway gear**

EYE-POPPING SUNGLASSES

To create your own eye-catching sunglasses, collect beads, sequins, silk flowers, old earrings, and other inexpensive ornamentation. Assemble these items in arrangements that particularly suit each girlfriend. One woman who is into aviation received a pair with tiny toy airplanes on the corners. Another who loves butterflies found them perched all over her rims. If you like to sail, use tiny plastic nautical flags. Use permanent glue to cover the frames of inexpensive sunglasses with your trinkets. Remember, the key to having fun with these treasures is to wear them collectively and with confidence. Happy sunning and strutting!

author put it, "together we form a chain, a chain of love reaching from the past into the future."[1]

This sense of being a part of something much bigger, and the strength that comes from that, is realized through a Girlfriends' Getaway. Regular participation in the lives of a small group of women results in knowledge about others and about yourself that may surprise you and certainly will enrich your life.

"I realized how safe I am around them and how genuine everyone is," revealed one getaway veteran. Another told us, "They've found out that I snore—and they love me anyway!" (We never said every discovery would be profound.)

The benefits come through no matter how simple or brief your getaway is. It doesn't have to be a full weekend in an exotic location. And according to one Girlfriends' Getaway participant, starting simple actually increases the chances of success. "Don't be overwhelmed; this doesn't have to be difficult," she counsels. "Having a Girlfriends' Getaway can be as simple as putting a pot of water on the stove for tea and taking the time to sit down and drink it. With your girlfriend, of course!"

Setting aside time, being intentional about investing in one another, getting together regularly—once a year, every six months, once a month—and being committed to one another. These are the core values of the Girlfriends' Getaway adventure. It's a time you can count on to spend with women you love. It matters little where you meet, how long it lasts, or how much (or little) it costs. What matters is that you're doing it!

When all is said and done, what is it that women really want (other than weekly maid service)? Author and world adventurer Barbara Jenkins asked women, and they told her. In her book *Wit and Wisdom for*

Women, Barbara collected quotes from women all over the world—simple women, wise women, strong women—women just like you. Here is a near-perfect description of what drives women to Girlfriends' Getaways: "The longer a woman lives, the more things she can successfully live without and continue to grow happier, except for love, family, and friends."[2] What women really want are friends they can confide in, friends they can trust, friends who offer consolation, friends they can love and enjoy. We couldn't agree more!

A LASTING BLESSING

Let's be honest. In today's rapidly changing world, we all need the safety net of tradition and the comfort of something—and someone—we can depend on. As you make Girlfriends' Getaways a regular part of your life, you'll form a tradition unlike any other, one that crosses lines of belief and background, a unique experience that you and your closest friends create together. It's a tradition that you'll never want to do without.

"Life is so short—time with your sisters can never be replaced or repeated," said one satisfied customer. And another, who pulls no punches, came up with this benediction: "If you have to wonder whether it's worth the effort…get new friends."

New friends, old friends, sisters, cousins. We need one another. That's the one thing we all agree on.

FIELD NOTES

Chapter 9

SHARE THE WEALTH

SHOULD YOU OPEN THE CIRCLE TO OTHERS?

It is possible to give away and become richer!
It is also possible to hold on too tightly and lose everything.
—PROVERBS 11:24 (TLB)

When we are fortunate enough to acquire something of great value, our first impulse is to hold it close. We fear that if we offer it freely to others, it might be greedily consumed and lost to us forever. We worry that if we allow others to handle it, it will lose its luster and diminish in value.

Although the beauty of this treasure enriches our lives, we hesitate to share it. If we extend this wonderful thing to others, they might not treat it with the care it deserves. Wouldn't it be wiser just to keep it to ourselves lest we forfeit this precious treasure?

This is the tension that our sisters face whenever we ask one another, "Is it time to invite others into the circle?" It's a question that will arise in nearly every Girlfriends' Getaway group, and the concerns are valid.

We confronted this struggle ourselves when, after a few years of Sisters Weekend bliss, our original group of mother and five sisters began to discuss the possibility of inviting other women to join us on our getaways. We started to feel the tug of "passing on" this treasure we had found. This was just too good to keep only for ourselves. But as we considered enlarging the circle, we began to wrestle with several questions. Who should we include? How large should the circle grow? How would the addition of new women change the experience?

Opening the circle to others would introduce significant changes in our annual adventure. Did we really want that? Every year we discussed these issues again, and each time we faced the same set of questions. What was best for the group, and what would be the best thing for those we considered inviting to join us?

THROUGH KATHLEEN'S EYES

I'm a charter member of our Sisters Weekend group, so I've known for more than a decade the richness that we savor whenever we get together. I felt so blessed to have something this special. But still, I wasn't sure I wanted to offer it to newcomers. "If we add new women to the group," I worried, "our experience wouldn't be the same." This rich blessing would no longer be ours alone. It would be changed, and maybe not for the better.

These emotions are real and understandable. But a danger lurks within them. If you become too attached to a treasured thing, its beauty can slowly diminish, and the joy you found in its discovery can ebb away. The ironic remedy is to share the wealth. Open your hands and just give it away! It's then that you find true fulfillment and realize that hoarding only keeps your treasure from shining—in your own life and in the lives of others. And who wants that?

So it was with great anticipation that, in the sixth year of our annual adventure, we extended an invitation to the next generation—our young adult daughters—to join us. The decision was not made lightly, because in some ways it was a sacrifice to include them. We knew our weekends would forever be altered, and there was a fear that our treasured sistering would be exchanged for mothering if daughters came along. We couldn't let that happen. The last thing we wanted to hear on our weekend was that beloved, but responsibility-laden, call word *"Mom!"*

Then we found a solution right in front of us, within our already established tradition. From the very beginning, a core element of our weekends has been that we leave our roles at home. There are no titles, no leaders, no followers. There is no hierarchy at all. The benefits of time *away* from being mothers and wives and employees and bosses and committee chairs are essential to the success of our time together. This isn't a weekend to fulfill duties or meet the expectations of others. By their very nature, our weekends are designed to get away from all that. We realized too that through the years our mom had never "mothered" us on our weekends but had participated equally in the sistering process. And so it would be with us after our daughters joined the group. Our tradition and the richness it brings wouldn't be sidetracked by opening the circle. The outside life of birth order and familial pecking order would continue to vanish once we left home, and the spirit of equality, acceptance, and frivolity would reign, as always.

Now, as each young woman of the next generation matures, she is invited to join us. She has the chance to see her grandmother, mother, aunts, and cousins in a new light. She experiences the freedom to explore being a woman in an environment of affirmation and safety while the rest of us have the opportunity to learn from and grow along with our younger sister.

Since we decided to open the circle of sisterhood, our weekends have developed a new dimension. Our annual adventures now enrich each successive generation, and tremendous bonds of friendship are being formed. We realize what we would have missed if we hadn't taken this new step along the path of adventure. The energy and spirit of our daughters and granddaughters have infused our weekends with new life, bringing a fresh perspective to everything from current events to fashion, music, books, even faith. Our shared getaways give us the chance to learn from one another in a way that we never envisioned. Instead of losing a precious treasure by extending it to our daughters, we found the joy of creating a priceless family legacy. And *that's* a far greater treasure than the one we started with!

THROUGH ELIZABETH'S EYES

I was one of the first two women of my generation to be initiated into Sisters Weekend. My cousin and I weren't prepared to enter a world in which our mothers, aunts, and grandmother step out from behind their familiar roles to enjoy one another as equals, as sisters, and as friends.

We now had a chance to see these women as partners in life-sharing and as creators of crazy fun. And once initiated, no young woman would ever want to be excluded from this sorority.

I was twenty-one, just starting my first job out of college and eager to be regarded as an independent and responsible adult. Was I in for a Sisters Weekend reality check! Little did I know that the words "responsible" and "adult" had no business showing up at *this* getaway. On my first night inside the circle of sisters, I couldn't believe my eyes. My elegant grandmother had completely forgotten that she was a dignified woman of seventy-three years. As we sat on the floor that first evening, my cousin and I looked up at a "regal" figure in all her glory. Before us sat my grandmother, but it appeared that she had completely forgotten what it meant to be a grandmother. Instead, she had transformed herself into Queen Moth-Hair. Her royal title found its origin in the paper-winged insects that made a comfortable home in her nest of hair. Queen Moth-Hair, who in real life was *Moth*-er to us all, began the evening's entertainment. And I don't use the word *entertainment* lightly.

She was a vision in ratty fake fur. Her crown: Burger King's finest cardboard. Her staff: wood from a swamp. Her jewels: machine-crafted in the back rooms of Wal-Mart. And only moments before she had simply been my grandma. I couldn't have been more surprised if she had told us she was running for president. I just sat on the floor, nearly stupefied by the scene that was unfolding, not sure what reaction was expected of me, but unable to display much more than a dumbfounded stare.

The queen's court soon followed, and I knew them well. In another life they were my mother and aunts. But suddenly, like Superwomen, they had been transformed into Little Dudettes. (I have no idea where the title came from. In the spirit of silliness, it was probably a spur-of-the-moment thing.) Five strong, they entered the royal chambers—what used to be a simple hotel bedroom—and proceeded to bestow gifts on my cousin and me, gifts nearly as precious as the royal trappings of Queen Moth-Hair herself! We received an assortment of odd and seemingly unrelated items, including a pair of obnoxiously decorated sunglasses, T-shirts proudly announcing our status as sisters, baseball caps adorned with various "jewels," and a silly aluminum ring, all signifying that we'd now become Little Dudettes ourselves. This was the scene of our initiation ceremony, doomed to be repeated as my other cousins came of age.

 getaway gear

FASHIONED IN UNITY

It's fun for everyone in your group to have her own Girlfriends' Getaway clothing. T-shirts are inexpensive, comfortable, and versatile. You can personalize them and then wear them as shirts, swimsuit cover-ups, or pj's.

To create your own fashion statement, first design a pattern or logo on cardboard that fits the name or personality of your girlfriends' group. You may want to use a favorite type font from your computer to get the right effect of size and spacing. Place the pattern *inside* the shirt so you can see it easily through the fabric. Then use a fabric pen or fabric paint and, following the directions on the package, trace over your pattern. Now wear your personalized T-shirts proudly, girlfriends!

As I write this a few years after the event, the ceremony seems normal enough. But at the time, I was far from prepared to be inducted into such an unconventional sorority. I mean, this was my *grandmother* wearing a Burger King crown and sporting paper moths in her hair. She never had been the prim, proper, boring grandmother-type, but neither had I ever seen her acting quite so, well, weird. I could accept my mom and aunts engaging in such nuttiness, but *my grandma?* Would I be expected to lose my inhibitions and act like this, too? I was an adult, after all. I didn't know if I had it in me to be that, well, weird.

I thought I had my dignity to maintain. Dignity shmignity!

By the time the initiation ceremony was over and we'd been handed all of our paraphernalia, my cousin and I had no choice but to shrug our shoulders and laugh, both at the scene before us and at ourselves. Yes, it was a great deal of fun and definitely a little, well, weird.

Now that I have several of these weekend adventures under my belt, what do I think? Most of all, I know I've found some of the best friends I could ask for. I've also noticed that an interesting thing happens when you throw together three generations of women who are open to learning from one another: A valuable process of mentoring occurs, and I don't mean just from older generations to younger.

Mentoring is a two-way street, which is what makes it different from simply setting an example. Real mentoring is a mutually respectful relationship built on a desire to teach and to learn. This kind of relationship is sadly lacking in our world. Older generations are not revered for their wisdom as they once were, and the younger generations are not respected or given much credit for their fresh insight and wisdom. As a result, we're all missing out on the wonderful gifts that these two groups can give to each other.

Women from an older generation may not know how to surf the Internet, and their idea of a Web site might be the crook in a tree branch, but have you ever stopped to look at a spider's web in the morning, sparkling with dew? I'll bet your grandmother has, and it's utterly breathtaking. So it is with our relationship with our elders. It can be a very beautiful thing, but it must be appreciated for the treasure that it is. We can't force it, but it often happens naturally when the circle of sisterhood convenes.

For example, I've discovered that my grandmother is one of the wisest people I know. Her wisdom comes not only from an inner calm that she possesses but also from simply having been around the block a few times. But if we didn't spend time together every year at Sisters Weekend, would we still be the glad beneficiaries of her hard-won wisdom? I wonder.

As for the younger generation, what do we have to offer our elders? We do have great depths of wisdom. The fresh eyes with which younger women see the world, yes even their naiveté, give them a unique perspective that is often discounted as unrealistic. It can be more real, however, than what the sometimes cynical and hardened "adult" eyes want to accept. Being with several generations of women reminds me that we all have something to learn from one another, regardless of age or experience.

It all comes from a foundation of respect. How do you acquire this respect? I believe it comes from appreciating people for who they are first, before seeing them as older or younger than you, wiser or more naive. It also comes from feeling safe enough to take a risk and reveal our true selves—our loves, passions, and dreams.

The first year my cousin and I attended Sisters Weekend, my grand-mother dressed up as one of her favorite singers, Patsy Cline, and sang to a recording of "Crazy." Grandma is a die-hard Patsy Cline fan, and she sang this somewhat melancholy song with great emotion. She took a risk doing that in front of all of us—we could have thought she was ready for "the home" or simply said, "Isn't that cute?" a little conde-scendingly. But we didn't. We thought it was a beautiful tribute, and we learned something about my grandma that we'd never known. It wasn't just that she loved Patsy Cline; it was that she was bold in sharing what she loved with the rest of us. She wanted her children and grandchildren to know who she really is. She wanted to share something that she treas-ured herself, a love for a great singer and the beauty of an emotion-packed song. Singing this song for us was an act of my grandmother's generosity and love. We felt we had learned something of the deeper parts of her soul, and we were honored.

It's a rare thing not to want to hide behind who you're supposed to be, and my respect for my grandmother grew that day, as did my love. I've seen a side of my grandmother that I would never have known otherwise. I received a tremendous gift that I treasure to this day.

EVERYONE WINS

We're not the only ones to see the benefits of enlarging the circle of sis-terhood to include different generations. After hearing about our Sisters Weekends, one of our friends put together a getaway with her mother, sister, and daughters. A few weeks before their weekend, one of her daughters confided a long-held desire: "I don't really know Grandma as a woman," she said. "I'd love to know how she overcame some of the tragedies in her life."

Our friend asked her mother if, during their getaway, she'd be willing to share about the three men in her life who had loved her. On their weekend, the grandmother told her daughters and granddaughters about each one of her husbands. She talked about their deaths and how losing them had affected her. She revealed her special strength, her courage, and her reliance on God. Our friend even learned things about the years she was growing up that she hadn't known before. It helped

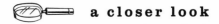 **a closer look**

WINNING AT LIFE

There is a group of women who call themselves the Wrestling Team. Interesting name, interesting women. Unlike some of the other groups we've introduced in this book, these ladies are not sisters by blood but by heart.

Their relationship began through tragic life circumstances. Each one of them has experienced deep pain through life-threatening illnesses or the loss of a spouse or child. The friend who first brought these women together noticed their common bond. She sensed their need to create a circle of sisterhood.

On their first getaway they talked about a name for the group. One of them said, "I tell people we're the Wrestling Team because we are always trying to sort things out and come to grips with the stuff in our lives as well as understand and accept God's plan for us." The name stuck.

her to understand her mother and herself better. Later that evening she presented her mother with a gift, a budding flower pin that symbolized the growth of the legacy she is passing on to the next generations.

We know another group of women—grandmother, mother, daughters, granddaughters—fourteen in all, ranging in age from ten to eighty-five, who gather yearly. Twenty-five years ago, their widowed grandma lost her sweetheart, and the next summer she asked her daughters to accompany her to a cottage on a lake. It would be their time to share memories and just be close as a family. It would be an experience that

---

And as they "wrestled" that first weekend, God blessed them. One of them told us, "He met us. He surrounded us with his love and met us in our laughter and fears. Our group melded closer, and we will never be the same as a result of friends being sisters together."

As we write this book, the Wrestling Team is beginning to widen its circle to include other women who need sistering, a new "generation" of women who want to explore life within the safety of friendship. These women have seen the value of "doing life together," and they want to pass on the benefits to others. They're willing to take new risks and expand their relationships with new friends. As they extend this blessing, they will continue to give away the treasure they've discovered and become richer through the eyes and hearts of their girlfriends.

---

would continue every year. What began in sadness has developed into a tradition of fun, laughter, support, and love. They tell us,

> We have gotten very close. We love and understand each other. Many times differences come up [understandable with fourteen women of such varied ages!], but we talk and work them out. It's a

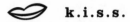 **k.i.s.s.**

MAKING A LARGER CIRCLE WORK

So you like the idea of opening the circle of sisterhood to include a few new-comers? If you're planning to bring together different generations, you may wonder how to bridge the age gap. Even if you're including new friends of roughly the same age, you still want them to feel they belong. Here are some pointers to consider.

- Don't focus on the roles of older/younger, wise/naive, or old friend/new friend. Instead, find common life experiences and share them. Try this for starters: Gather pictures of each girlfriend at the same age and talk about your memories. Tell about your best friend, about your favorite thing to do on the weekend at that age, and about your childhood sweetheart. Add your own questions.
- Play a game such as "Chicken Soup for the Soul" (a board game based on the best-selling book series), which asks probing questions. You'll be surprised and delighted by what you learn about one another.

---

great experience getting to know each other on our own terms with many different nuances of personality.

Just like our friends, each one of us, no matter what generation we're part of, has learned and grown from our shared weekends. We've all been blessed by one another, and the strength we feel as a group of

---

- Shopping can bridge a gap like nothing else! This is a chance for your younger friends to be the teachers. Take your group to your favorite makeup counter and show them what you like in the latest trends. We bet your girlfriends will appreciate any help in keeping up-to-date.
- If you're planning meals, team up older and younger or veteran and newer girlfriends. This will provide some time of intimate interaction and creativity between just two or three friends.
- Recommend a book that you've read that has had an impact on your life.
- Share music that touches your heart or that challenges or inspires you because of the lyrics, because of the time in your life when the song was popular, or because of the people who come to mind when you hear this song. Here's a great opportunity for members of different generations to learn from and about one another.

---

women united is like nothing else in our lives. We didn't lose anything when we opened the circle to the next generation. We gained depth and breadth. The joy, the support, and the shared wisdom now flow back and forth between generations.

You and your girlfriends at some point will ask the question: "Should we open the circle of sisters to others?" Here's the answer, in almost every case: "Absolutely!"

FIELD NOTES

The adventure continues

WHETHER FOR A WEEKEND OR A MOMENT,
THERE IS STRENGTH IN SISTERING

The end of all our exploring will be to arrive where we started and to know the place for the first time. —T. S. ELIOT

You've now gone on your first Girlfriends' Getaway? What did you think? Our greatest hope is that you had such a wonderful time that you're already planning your next adventure. But you don't have to wait an entire year for another getaway. You can set aside meaningful moments with your circle of sisters whenever and wherever you need them.

A Girlfriends' Getaway, in the fullest sense, is a planned-for, extended time to concentrate on being together with your closest friends. But what about all those other times when you hit a rough spot in life and only your girlfriend can provide what you need? You know these times: when the dreaded pink slip lands on your desk, when the dog has fleas and the baby has diaper rash, when the boyfriend tells you he enlisted and is leaving tomorrow...well, you get the picture. Those are the times when you need to have a Girlfriends' Getaway Moment.

Yes, a Getaway *Moment*. We think it's the most wonderful thing since color-fast lipstick. It's a short time—an hour, an evening, a lunch—when you can re-create the getaway experience without the full getaway time commitment. You can connect with your girlfriends when you really need them on the spur of the moment. Whether it calls for a coffee break, lunch at your favorite restaurant, or an impromptu spa night (see appendix 3), the Getaway Moment, like the full Girlfriends' Getaway, is yours to design for yourself and your girlfriends.

So how is this different from any other simple get-together, you ask? A Girlfriends' Getaway Moment is a precious, but not necessarily rare, event. It fills you up, keeps you going, and gives you hope and encouragement. You take the trust and bonding you've created during your extended getaways and you bring them to your Getaway Moment. When you tell your girlfriend that you need a Getaway Moment, she'll know exactly what you're talking about and how to be there for you—and vice versa, when she needs special time with you. It's when life and relationships among women really happen. Take time for moments like these, for they are the ones you'll remember and cling to.

And then there are the plans for next year's getaway. This adventure of girlfriends investing in one another's lives isn't meant to be a one-time event that you return to only as a pleasant memory when ever you flip through your photo album. It's an adventure that continues in your own life and in the lives of your friends. It's up to you to keep it going and to live it, for in your relationships with your girlfriends you'll find the true adventure of life, which is love and support, listening and enjoying. Your story will inspire others, just as we hope ours inspired you.

We're thrilled that you've joined the circle of girlfriends. This is just the beginning, you know. The adventure goes on…

GIRLFRIENDS' GETAWAY RESOURCES

GAMES, GEAR, GADGETS, AND GOOFINESS

Think good thoughts, be ready to party,
and share laughter and love with each other.
—GIRLFRIENDS' GETAWAY VETERAN

When people hear about our weekend adventures, one of their first questions is, "What do you *do?*" The best answer is: "What *don't* we do?" We enjoy going out on the town for dinners and plays. We go shopping and exploring. But our favorite moments are often the ones we create for ourselves. There's nothing that can entertain us quite as well as we can!

We encourage you to make your Girlfriends' Getaway totally unique. Don't rely on the tried and true. Instead of being entertained, come up with ways to entertain yourselves!

Warning: Don't be tempted to bring along too much gear, and be careful not to plan such elaborate productions that you'll all feel burdened rather than refreshed. This is a time for relaxation and letting go, not a work shift.

WHEN WE WERE KIDS

This is a fun evening event. Get ready to turn back the clock and revisit yourself when you were less than five feet tall and still played with Barbies. Not only is going back to childhood good fun, for most of us it hearkens to a simpler time. Get cozy around the fireplace or bonfire, surround yourselves with munchies (we have some suggestions below) and music, and you'll be set until the wee hours.

If you've known one another since childhood, think back to the first time you met or the first class you had together. Who was the teacher? Who else sat in your row? What games did you play during recess or gym? Remember what life was like back then and re-create it through your memories. This also works if you met in high school or college.

If your friendships date to the more recent past, you can still entertain one another with girlhood stories. Some of you might not know much about one another's childhood, so sit in a circle and have each friend describe her first date, her first kiss, or some other rite of passage. Share your strongest childhood memory, a turning point in your life, the moment you really understood that you were *alive*. This is powerful and wonderful not only for your girlfriends, but for you, too. You may recall things about yourself that you'd forgotten. You could rediscover a you that has been missing for long time!

No matter which tack you take, this is a fun, nonthreatening way to begin to establish the bonds of sisterhood.

Good Things to Eat

If a kitchen comes with your Girlfriends' Getaway accommodations, plan meals that are simple, quick, and fun to eat. If you want, each girlfriend can prepare a meal that hearkens back to childhood or to a shared experience from the past. We've included a few of our own recipes to get you thinking. Give some of these a try, or stick to what you know and love. Just keep it simple, sister, and have fun!

Banana and Brown Sugar Sandwiches

Kathleen and her sisters love these because their mom served them for lunch when they were kids. We've never found anyone else who has heard of them. Yes, they're weird, but they're yummy!

2 slices of white bread, buttered

½ banana, sliced lengthwise

1 teaspoon brown sugar sprinkled on banana

Make sandwich with ingredients and cut in quarters.

Open-Face Grilled Cheese Sandwiches

These are easy to make and good to eat.

White bread slices (what else?)

Velveeta cheese slices (this is a recipe from the '50s and '60s), one
cheese slice per bread slice

Place on cookie sheet or broiler pan. Place under broiler until lightly bubbled and toasted. Serve immediately.

Fruit Salad

This one's as easy as one, two, three!

1 large can mixed fruit, drained

1 banana, sliced

1 cup petite marshmallows

Cool Whip

Fold the ingredients together in a large bowl and serve chilled. (Okay, maybe it's one, two, three, four, five, but who's counting?)

Candy Cookies

If you have candy lovers in your group (and who doesn't), make these ahead of time.

In a pan stir together and bring to a boil:

1 cup white sugar

1 cup white Karo syrup

Remove from stove and add, mixing well:

¾ cup peanut butter

1 teaspoon vanilla

3 cups corn flakes

Butter a 9 x 12" pan and spread mixture evenly. In pan, on low heat melt:

½ package chocolate chips

½ package caramel chips

Spread mixture on top of bars. Chill slightly before cutting into small squares. Warning: These are very rich. A little goes a long way!

PERSONALIZED ENTERTAINMENT

These activities will delight your girlfriends and make you all feel like kids again!

Picture Place Cards

Not only are these personal and welcoming, but they provide a delightful reminder of how cute you all were! Copy childhood (not baby) photos in black and white. Glue them to three-by-five-inch index cards. Trim to a shape or use them as rectangles. Glue an index-card triangle to the back so you can stand the photo up and use it as a place card. What better way to welcome your girlfriends to the gathering!

Candy Favors

Look in your specialized candy store for what we used to call "penny candy"—candy bracelets, necklaces, suckers, and so forth. Package a selection of sweets in colorful paper napkins tied with red string licorice "ribbon," and set one at each plate. How sweet it is!

Great Music

Play songs that evoke memories of your childhood era: Scores from Disney movies, show tunes, *Sesame Street* songs, or anything that's fun and girly, such as Maurice Chevalier singing "Thank Heaven for Little Girls." Check your library for soundtracks, kids' music, oldies, and the like. Tip: Music is key to setting a mood, but you'll soon tire of children's tunes. Have a variety of styles available that everyone will enjoy.

Show and Tell

Remember this little public exercise from back in grade school? Well, it's time to make Show and Tell fun again by doing it with your girlfriends. Use the suggestions in chapter 6 to prompt some memories worth telling about. Or show movies, slides, or picture albums that have a personal meaning for you. Make it fun and silly, and Show and Tell will soon be something you'll look forward to!

HOITY-TOITY NIGHT

This is a new and welcome addition to our own Sisters Weekend getaways. We can't even say it anymore without laughing. It's easy to do and an ideal choice for girlfriends staying in a hotel room or at home. Pinkies up, girls, we're going "over the top" tonight!

THE EVENING MENU

- Sparkling punch
- Cheese and crackers
- Frozen grapes
- Gourmet chocolates

Sparkling Punch
1 can of white grape juice concentrate
1 can of apple juice concentrate
2 two-liter bottles of ginger ale or lemon-lime soda

Mix ingredients in a punch bowl and add orange and lemon slices (or edible flowers, if you like).

Cheese and Crackers
Go to a gourmet store and choose a variety of cheeses and crackers. Arrange on a platter with a fresh cut flower or two. (Don't forget to bring cheese knives.)

Frozen Grapes
Frozen grapes are incredibly refreshing and beautiful. They almost look like frosted glass. Wash, dry, then freeze red and green grapes. Place on a silver platter with a few white flowers. If you can't keep the grapes frozen, don't worry, they'll be okay. If you can't freeze them, make it simple and serve them just as they are.

Gourmet Chocolates
A box or two of your favorite varieties arranged on a plate will delight everyone! When it comes to chocolate, the fresh cut flower is optional.

THE EVENING DRESS

- black dress—simple, elegant, classic
- jewels (These don't have to be simple, elegant, or classic; this is where the hoity toity comes in. Dig out your family costume jewelry or buy candy rings for a substitute.)
- long gloves (You probably haven't worn them since prom! Take them off before you eat the chocolate.)
- feather boas (You can find them at fabric stores.)

- the most elegant hats you have
- paper fans
- tulle (It's inexpensive, lightweight, and comes in pretty colors. You can wrap the table or yourself in it.)

Music

- The Three Tenors—ahhh, opera! (or, eeek, opera! depending on your taste in music)
- anything by Cole Porter
- "Diamonds Are a Girl's Best Friend" and other hoity-toity tunes from the glamour era
- recordings of any other music that appeals to you—as long as it makes you feel hoity and toity! And if the spirit moves you, get up and dance!

Movies

Take a break from conversation. Watch a Fred Astaire and Ginger Rogers movie such as *Top Hat* or *Flying Down to Rio*. As you watch their graceful moves, remind yourself that Ginger did everything Fred did only backwards and in high heels!

Decor

- Add a little water to clear plastic cups. Place a tea light in it (not a votive; tea lights are safer). Add gold or silver confetti glitter. Or, if you can't burn candles, hang a string of tiny white twinkle lights. Just keep the room lights low. Remember to bring an extension cord.

- Dress up paper plates with gold or silver paper doilies.
- Use gold or silver paper napkins.
- Drink from fancy stemware. (Glass is best, but plastic will do in a pinch.)
- If you are in a hotel room, turn your bathroom sink and counter into a wet bar. Plug the drain, fill the sink with ice and nestle your drinks in the ice. Set out glasses or cups, sugar cubes, and lemon slices. Roll up gold and silver paper napkins and tuck them in glasses. Scatter confetti glitter on the counter and place several candles around for added sparkle. Turn off the lights.

CONVERSATIONS

Try these ideas to start enjoyable, and sometimes revealing, conversations.

- Ask, What was the most glamorous night of your life?
- See who can do the best Audrey Hepburn or Queen Elizabeth impression.
- Anyone know French? Give a simple lesson.
- In true hoity-toity spirit, attempt to answer the age-old question: Are diamonds really a girl's best friend? (Marilyn's opinion notwithstanding.)

DO-IT-YOURSELF
Day Spa

Get ready to pamper one another! Set out a table with plenty of towels and a few candles, put on bathrobes and slippers, and prepare for an evening of true indulgence. Or make spa time an all-day event, beginning with a brisk walk. Have a smoothie afterward, put on the hair mask, and begin your facial. Follow up with showers and a light lunch. Then do afternoon manicures and pedicures. By the time you're finished, you'll all be ready for a night on the town!

FACIAL

Always begin a facial with squeaky-clean skin! Use the Strawberry Oatmeal Scrub described below or simply use your favorite cleanser. The general order of a facial is cleanser, mask, toner, and moisturizer.

Strawberry Oatmeal Scrub

"Scrub" is really a misnomer; you should never scrub your face. Always be gentle! This can be made ahead of time and kept cool. One recipe is enough for three women.

2 tablespoons rolled oats

3 large, ripe strawberries, no stems or leaves

1 teaspoon milk

Grind the oats into a fine powder using a blender or coffee bean grinder (a clean one). Mash the strawberries and mix with oats. Add enough milk to make a paste. Lightly massage into skin and rinse. The fruit acids in the strawberries will remove dead surface cells, while the milk and oats soothe your skin.

Moisturizing Avocado Mask

If you're hungry in the morning, you can even eat this! But save some for your face—it does wonders. This is good for dry, mature, or sensitive skin. It makes enough for two masks.

1 tablespoon honey

½ ripe avocado, peeled and pitted

1 tablespoon plain yogurt

In a blender or food processor, puree ingredients until smooth. Slather onto face (don't skimp) and leave on three to five minutes. Take a group photo. Rinse. This mask can be made ahead of time. Just be sure to keep it refrigerated until you use it!

Papaya Mud Mask

This is Elizabeth's favorite mask ever; she doesn't use store-bought masks now that she's discovered this simple one. It's great for any skin type, but especially oily, breakout-prone skin. This recipe makes enough for about three masks.

> *½ papaya*
>
> *Fuller's earth or kaolin clay (optional) (Look for these products in the beauty section of your health food store. They give the mask some thickness and help it to stay on your face better.)*

Seed the papaya and scoop out the flesh. Mix with a tablespoon of clay, adding more until you get a thick, but not dry, consistency. Spread on your face and leave on no more than ten minutes. If the clay begins to dry, rinse it off. You'll have smooth skin to rival a baby's bottom!

Rosewater Toner

This is actually very easy and very indulgent. It makes enough for at least ten girlfriends.

> *Petals from one rose*
>
> *1 cup boiling water, preferably distilled*

Pour boiling water over the rose petals to make a great facial steam. Put a towel over your head and let the aroma and gentle oils soothe your senses and your skin. Resist the temptation to linger, however. No more than ten minutes of steam time, and less if you have broken capillaries. When the water is cool, filter out the petals and bottle the rose-scented water. Use as a toner by applying to your face with cotton after your mask.

Herbal Toner

Use the herb of your choice. We recommend lavender for all skin types, chamomile for dry skin, and mint or parsley for oily skin.

> *1 cup boiling water*

Prepare and use as you would the rosewater.

Light Moisturizer

This is enough for five faces.

> *1 tablespoon aloe vera gel*
>
> *1 drop essential oil, such as rose, chamomile, or lavender*

Combine gel with essential oil and apply to face and body after toner. Aloe vera is naturally healing and wonderful for sunburned skin.

Mayo and Avocado Hair Mask

This is just like a mask for your face, but you put it on your hair instead. It adds body and shine and conditions deeply. It's especially great if you've been swimming in a chlorine-treated pool. It makes enough for at least five masks.

> *1 ripe avocado*
>
> *1 cup mayonnaise*

Blend ingredients together until smooth. Apply liberally to hair and leave on for twenty minutes. Shampoo out. This is best used either in the morning or at the beginning of your spa night, as it takes a while to work its magic and will do no harm if left on your hair longer than twenty minutes. Take turns shampooing one another's hair in the sink. Spread the remainder on sandwiches. (Just kidding, but you really could!)

PEDICURE

Fizzy Foot Soak

> *2 drops essential oil, such as lemon, ginger, or peppermint*
>
> *3 tablespoon baking soda*
>
> *1 tablespoon citric acid (sold in health food stores)*

This is so much fun, but is only worth doing with a small group, as each person must have her own foot tub and complete recipe. Fill the tub with the warmest water you can stand, add the essential oil, then the soda and citric acid together. They react and make bubbles that will tickle and massage your feet.

Peppermint Foot Lotion
One recipe is enough for one person.
> *3 tablespoons unscented lotion (enough for your feet and calves)*
> *5 drops peppermint essential oil*

Why pay premium for store-bought peppermint lotion when you can make your own? Thoroughly mix the essential oil with the lotion and you've got the coolingest cool mint concoction around.

MANICURE

All you need for a great manicure is some liquid castille soap (we prefer Dr. Bronner's) and water, some apricot kernel oil, and a nail buffer. Rub the oil into your cuticles, soak your fingers in the soapy water, and buff those babies to a high shine! If you want to enjoy the softest hands since Palmolive, try this sugar rub: Mix equal parts sugar and olive oil and rub into hands. Rinse with warm water (no soap!) and pat dry. This is wonderful for feet, too. Do it before bed and then put on cotton socks. You won't believe your feet could be so soft!

SPA CUISINE

These smoothies all make enough for two.

Creamy Orange Smoothie
1 frozen banana, sliced (you might want to slice it before you freeze it)
1 cup orange juice or 3 tablespoons frozen concentrate
½ cup vanilla frozen or regular yogurt

Blend until smooth; garnish with a slice of orange. Optional: add protein powder or psyllium husks (fiber) for added spalike goodness!

Mango Mint Smoothie (Elizabeth's favorite)
1 cup frozen mango chunks
2 tablespoons fresh mint leaves
½ cup vanilla yogurt, frozen or regular

Blend until smooth and garnish with a mint leaf.

Lemon-Cucumber Water
Slice half a cucumber and half a lemon and place in a pitcher. Fill with water and chill. This is guaranteed to be the most refreshing water you've ever had! Just replace the fruit every couple of days.

A Note on Essential Oils
You may notice that essential oils play heavily in the spa recipes above. There is a good reason for that. Since essential oils are just what their name implies, essences of the plants from which they are derived, they contain highly concentrated, highly beneficial properties. Some of these properties are unique solely to the essential oil, as it often takes several hundred pounds of plant material to make one pound of essential oil. This is why essential oils are sometimes quite pricey. The value comes in having a product that is completely natural and quite powerful. A little goes a long way. If you're going to invest in any essential oils, don't waste

them by taking the dropper off the top (you know you have a good quality oil if it has a built-in dropper) and dumping the oil into whatever you're making. Not only will you ruin the recipe, as nothing needs or can take that much essential oil, but you also will have thrown your money away.

When buying an oil, be sure each one has its own price. Each oil costs a different amount to produce. Lavender, for example, is a reasonably low-priced oil, while rose is one of the most expensive. Also, don't confuse essential oils with scented oils. The latter are synthetic and have no business going anywhere near your face.

Drop by your nearest health food store and sample a few essential oils. Inhale several different fragrances and see which types you like the best. Our guess is that you won't be able to leave without buying at least one!

ROOM FRESHENER

For a handmade room freshening spray, add a few drops of lemon, orange, and peppermint oils to distilled water and place in a spray bottle. This fragrant mixture will mask any unpleasantness, if you know what we mean!

BUG REPELLENT

3 drops citronella or lemongrass
3 drops rosemary
3 drops peppermint

Add to 8 ounces of distilled water or a light oil such as apricot kernel or grapeseed, and apply all over skin!

Your Time in the Sun

During your spa day, you may want to spend some time at the pool or just lying in the sun. But don't forget the sunscreen! Thanks to ozone depletion, you need sunscreen every day. Does this mean you have to be a pale ghost all summer? No way! In addition to burning away half our atmosphere, modern living has also brought to life a new generation of self-tanners that really work. They're not going to turn you orange, we promise! We prefer Neutrogena Sunless Tanning Spray and Clarins self-tanner. Both go on easily and leave you looking nicely golden.

Here are a few things to remember from those of us who have lived with the dreaded streaks. First, apply tanner onto freshly shaved legs. If you have stubble, the tanner tends to collect around the hairs and you end up with polka dots. Second, rub the tanner in a circular motion, not up and down your arms or legs. This is how you end up streaky. Blend the tanner all the way up your thighs and down to your feet (or up to your shoulders and down to your hands), and apply sparingly to knees, ankles, and elbows. Third, never put tanner on your face, unless the package specifically says "for face." Even then, you're taking a chance that the tiniest mistake will be there where you can't hide it and can't remove it. Instead, opt for a nice bronzer that will wash off with soap and water.

Tips for Instant Beauty

One of our sisters has just about every type of makeup known to woman. She hauled (and we mean *hauled*) it all to one of our Sisters Weekends, and we did makeovers and traded beauty secrets. These are some of our best:

- Sunscreen, sunscreen, sunscreen. Or carry a colorful sun umbrella. (Okay, this isn't really a secret, but it's the best way to keep you looking and feeling beautiful!)
- Highlight your hair—all-over color, especially dark, is aging and unnatural.
- Eyebrows—well-shaped brows make your whole face come alive. Use an eyebrow brush and eye shadow powder rather than pencil; it creates a softer, more natural look.
- Smile a lot; it always makes you look younger. To enhance that smile, experiment with a new shade of lipstick: for rosy complexions, stick with rosy, berry colors; for olive or golden complexions, use orange and brown tones.
- Try the Girlfriends' Getaway Instant Diet: good posture! Stand up straight, tummy in, shoulders back and down. You'll instantly look ten pounds lighter. If you want to see an example of perfect posture, check out Audrey Hepburn in *Sabrina,* or in any of her other movies—incredible!
- Be adventurous—don't get in a rut with your beauty routine. Try something new, experiment, and have fun with it!

For detailed, professional tips and an out-of-the-box approach to makeup, check out the books *Making Faces* (Little, Brown, & Co., 1997) and *Face Forward* (Little, Brown, & Co., 2000), both by Kevyn Aucoin. For a more natural, subtle look, consult *Bobbi Brown Beauty: The Ultimate Beauty Resource,* by Bobbi Brown (HarperCollins, 1997).

FAST FOOD THAT GIRLFRIENDS LOVE

Here are some quick and easy recipes that we really love. We're sure you will, too!

Creamy Salsa Dip

8 oz. package of cream cheese

1 cup salsa, or to taste

Soften cream cheese in the microwave and mix in the salsa. That's it! Even a two-year-old could make this stuff, and it's great with chips or veggies.

Chicken Roll-Ups

2 cups ground chicken (canned will work)

1 cucumber, thinly sliced

1 cup grated cheese, your choice
4 flour tortillas

Mix the chicken with a little mayo to taste and spread on the tortillas, covering the entire surface (not just down the middle). Cover with a layer of cucumbers and sprinkle cheese on top (not too much). Roll up like a scroll, not like a burrito, and slice into half-inch slices. Makes a delicious and deceptively intricate-looking appetizer. Variation: substitute the chicken with cream cheese and eliminate the grated cheese—simple, quick, and yummy!

Gourmet Pizza

Assemble your favorite toppings and bake according to pizza crust directions.

1 premade pizza crust
1 avocado
chihuahua cheese, grated (or substitute your favorite)
tomatoes, fresh or sun-dried
cilantro to taste

Variation # 1:
fresh mozzarella
sun-dried tomatoes
basil
olive oil and balsamic vinegar drizzled on top

Variation #2:
Make your favorite salad and pile it on top of the pizza crust—great
for warm weather!

Strawberries in Balsamic Vinegar (think sweet and sour)

   2 tablespoons brown sugar

   2 tablespoons balsamic vinegar

   1 quart strawberries

Mix the sugar and vinegar together and add strawberries. It's a bizarre combination, but one we think you'll love.

CHAPTER 1

1. Renee E. Spraggins, "Women in the United States, A Profile." U.S. Census Brief. U.S. Department of Commerce, Economics, and Statistics Administration and U.S. Census Bureau, March 2000.

2. Ginny Graves, "Women M.D.s Speak: Get Your Cholesterol Tested This Year," *Self,* February 2000, 37.

3. Ericka McConnel, "The Idea Is Comfort," *O, The Oprah Magazine,* February 2000, 110.

CHAPTER 4

1. Nicole Johnson, *Fresh-Brewed Life: A Stirring Invitation to Wake Up Your Soul* (Nashville: Nelson, 1999), 66.

CHAPTER 6

1. Barbara Jenkins, *Wit and Wisdom for Women: How to Stay on Track in These Fast Times* (Nashville: Nelson, 1996), 110.

2. See Gregory Stock, Ph.D., *The Book of Questions* (New York: Workman Publishing, 1985).

3. Ruth Haley Barton, *Becoming a Woman of Strength,* Revised Edition (Wheaton: Harold Shaw, 1999), 71.

CHAPTER 7

1. Taken from Autumn Stephens, *Out of the Mouths of Babes: Quips and Quotes from Wildly Witty Women* (Berkeley, Calif.: Conari Press, 2000), 262.

CHAPTER 8

1. Ellyn Sanna, *Just the Girls: A Celebration of Mothers and Daughters* (Uhrichsville, Ohio: Barbour, 2000), 6.

2. Barbara Jenkins, *Wit and Wisdom for Women: How to Stay on Track in These Fast Times* (Nashville: Nelson, 1996), 113.

KATHLEEN LAING has two daughters, Elizabeth and Jennifer, and has been married thirty-two years to her husband, Craig. She has experience in interior design and modeling and is a former staff member of Willow Creek Community Church outside Chicago. This is her first book.

ELIZABETH BUTTERFIELD is Kathleen's daughter and is a mother herself. She has been married five years to her husband, Kirk. She was a flight attendant for several years and is now a full-time mother and writer. Both she and Kathleen live in the Minneapolis area. This is also Elizabeth's first book.

To learn more about WaterBrook Press and view
our catalog of products, log on to our Web site:
www.waterbrookpress.com

WATERBROOK
PRESS